W9-DBI-685

Leadership Abroad Begins at Home

Integrating National Economies: Promise and Pitfalls

Barry Bosworth (Brookings Institution) and Gur Ofer (Hebrew University)
Reforming Planned Economies in an Integrating World Economy

Ralph C. Bryant (Brookings Institution)
International Coordination of National Stabilization Policies

Susan M. Collins (Brookings Institution/Georgetown University)
Distributive Issues: A Constraint on Global Integration

Richard N. Cooper (Harvard University)
Environment and Resource Policies for the World Economy

Ronald G. Ehrenberg (Cornell University)
Labor Markets and Integrating National Economies

Barry Eichengreen (University of California, Berkeley)
International Monetary Arrangements for the 21st Century

Mitsuhiro Fukao (Bank of Japan)
Financial Integration, Corporate Governance, and the Performance of Multinational Companies

Stephan Haggard (University of California, San Diego)
Developing Nations and the Politics of Global Integration

Richard J. Herring (University of Pennsylvania) and Robert E. Litan (Department of Justice/Brookings Institution)
Financial Regulation in the Global Economy

Miles Kahler (University of California, San Diego)
International Institutions and the Political Economy of Integration

Anne O. Krueger (Stanford University)
Trade Policies and Developing Nations

Robert Z. Lawrence (Harvard University)
Regionalism, Multilateralism, and Deeper Integration

Sylvia Ostry (University of Toronto) and Richard R. Nelson (Columbia University)
Techno-Nationalism and Techno-Globalism: Conflict and Cooperation

Robert L. Paarlberg (Wellesley College/Harvard University)
Leadership Abroad Begins at Home: U.S. Foreign Economic Policy after the Cold War

Peter Rutland (Wesleyan University)
Russia, Eurasia, and the Global Economy

F. M. Scherer (Harvard University)
Competition Policies for an Integrated World Economy

Susan L. Shirk (University of California, San Diego)
How China Opened Its Door: The Political Success of the PRC's Foreign Trade and Investment Reforms

Alan O. Sykes (University of Chicago)
Product Standards for Internationally Integrated Goods Markets

Akihiko Tanaka (Institute of Oriental Culture, University of Tokyo)
The Politics of Deeper Integration: National Attitudes and Policies in Japan

Vito Tanzi (International Monetary Fund)
Taxation in an Integrating World

William Wallace (St. Antony's College, Oxford University)
Regional Integration: The West European Experience

Robert L. Paarlberg

Leadership Abroad Begins at Home

U. S. Foreign Economic Policy after the Cold War

Andrew Carnegie Library
Livingstone College
701 W. Monroe St.
Salisbury, NC 28144

THE BROOKINGS INSTITUTION
Washington, D.C.

126540

Copyright © 1995
THE BROOKINGS INSTITUTION
1775 Massachusetts Avenue, N. W., Washington, D.C. 20036

All rights reserved

Library of Congress Cataloging-in-Publication data:
Robert L. Paarlberg
Leadership abroad begins at home: U. S. foreign economic
policy after the Cold War/Robert L. Paarlberg
p. cm. — (Integrating national economies)
Includes bibliographical references and index.
ISBN 0-8157-6804-4 (alk. paper) — ISBN 0-8157-6803-6
(pbk: alk. paper)
1. United States—Foreign economic relations.
2. United States—Economic policy—1993–
I. Title. II. Series.

HF1455.P2 1995   94-34565
337.73—dc20   CIP

9 8 7 6 5 4 3 2 1

The paper used in this publication meets the minimum requirements of
American National Standard for Information Sciences—Permanence of Paper
for Printed Library Materials, ANSI Z39.48-1984

Typeset in Plantin

Composition by Princeton Editorial Associates
Princeton, New Jersey

Printed by R. R. Donnelley and Sons Co.
Harrisonburg, Virginia

ᛒ THE BROOKINGS INSTITUTION

The Brookings Institution is an independent organization devoted to nonpartisan research, education, and publication in economics, government, foreign policy, and the social sciences generally. Its principal purposes are to aid in the development of sound public policies and to promote public understanding of issues of national importance.

The Institution was founded on December 8, 1927, to merge the activities of the Institute for Government Research, founded in 1916, the Institute of Economics, founded in 1922, and the Robert Brookings Graduate School of Economics and Government, founded in 1924.

The Board of Trustees is responsible for the general administration of the Institution, while the immediate direction of the policies, program, and staff is vested in the President, assisted by an advisory committee of the officers and staff. The by-laws of the Institution state: "It is the function of the Trustees to make possible the conduct of scientific research, and publication, under the most favorable conditions, and to safeguard the independence of the research staff in the pursuit of their studies and in the publication of the results of such studies. It is not a part of their function to determine, control, or influence the conduct of particular investigations or the conclusions reached."

The President bears final responsibility for the decision to publish a manuscript as a Brookings book. In reaching his judgment on the competence, accuracy, and objectivity of each study, the President is advised by the director of the appropriate research program and weighs the views of a panel of expert outside readers who report to him in confidence on the quality of the work. Publication of a work signifies that it is deemed a competent treatment worthy of public consideration but does not imply endorsement of conclusions or recommendations.

The Institution maintains its position of neutrality on issues of public policy in order to safeguard the intellectual freedom of the staff. Hence interpretations or conclusions in Brookings publications should be understood to be solely those of the authors and should not be attributed to the Institution, to its trustees, officers, or other staff members, or to the organizations that support its research.

Board of Trustees

James A. Johnson
Chairman

Leonard Abramson
Ronald J. Arnault
Rex J. Bates
A. W. Clausen
John L. Clendenin
D. Ronald Daniel
Walter Y. Elisha
Stephen Friedman
William H. Gray III

Vartan Gregorian
Teresa Heinz
Samuel Hellman
Warren Hellman
Robert A. Helman
Thomas W. Jones
Vernon E. Jordan, Jr.
James A. Joseph
Breene M. Kerr
Thomas G. Labrecque
Donald F. McHenry

Bruce K. MacLaury
David O. Maxwell
Constance Berry Newman
Maconda Brown O'Connor
Samuel Pisar
Rozanne L. Ridgway
David Rockefeller, Jr.
Michael P. Schulhof
Robert H. Smith
John D. Zeglis
Ezra K. Zilkha

Honorary Trustees

Elizabeth E. Bailey
Vincent M. Barnett, Jr.
Barton M. Biggs
Louis W. Cabot
Edward W. Carter
Frank T. Cary
William T. Coleman, Jr.
Lloyd N. Cutler
Kenneth W. Dam
Bruce B. Dayton
Douglas Dillon
Charles W. Duncan, Jr.

Robert F. Erburu
Robert D. Haas
Andrew Heiskell
Roger W. Heyns
Roy M. Huffington
Nannerl O. Keohane
James T. Lynn
William McC. Martin, Jr.
Robert S. McNamara
Mary Patterson McPherson
Arjay Miller
Donald S. Perkins

J. Woodward Redmond
Charles W. Robinson
James D. Robinson III
Howard D. Samuel
B. Francis Saul II
Ralph S. Saul
Henry B. Schacht
Robert Brookings Smith
Morris Tanenbaum
John C. Whitehead
James D. Wolfensohn

Foreword

A FTER World War II and during the cold war, U.S. leadership was critical to Western security and to the creation of a more deeply integrated world economy. Now that the cold war has ended, the focus of U.S. policy may turn inward. If so, will deeper international economic integration be placed at risk?

In this book, Robert Paarlberg asserts that leadership by the United States remains important to global economic integration, yet he proposes a new leadership style better suited to post–cold war realities. U.S. economic cooperation with nations abroad can no longer be founded on a common security threat, U.S. economic hegemony has diminished, and the outward-oriented executive branch has less influence over an inward-oriented Congress. These new circumstances have revived the importance of some more traditional impediments to outward-oriented U.S. policy leadership, including divided government, discontinuity and division in the executive branch, federalism, and cultural insularity.

Under these circumstances, asserts Paarlberg, it may be appropriate for the United States to attempt fewer policy initiatives abroad and to concentrate first on putting wise economic policies in place at home. Acting first at home, says the author, need not lead to protectionism, isolationism, or even unilateralism. International cooperation abroad can be made easier if sound policies are already in place at home. Paarlberg illustrates this proposition with case studies in international fiscal policy coordination, agricultural policy reform, and international environmental policy.

The author wishes to acknowledge the assistance of many persons in the writing of this book. He is particularly grateful to the series editors Henry J. Aaron, Ralph C. Bryant, Susan M. Collins, and Robert Z. Lawrence for their tolerant support of an argument that cuts somewhat across the grain of internationalist traditions. Helpful substantive comments on earlier drafts were made by Lawrence Broz, I. M. Destler, Jeffry A. Frieden, C. Randall Henning, Stanley Hoffmann, Robert Keohane, Robert J. Lieber, Craig Murphy, Henry Nau, Pietro S. Nivola, Eric Nordlinger, John Odell, Roger B. Porter, Robert Putnam, Vito Tanzi, and Raymond Vernon. The Department of Political Science at Wellesley College and the Harvard Center for International Affairs provided institutional support.

Samuel Allen edited the manuscript, Jason D. Rhoades verified it, and Sara Hufham provided administrative support. Princeton Editorial Associates prepared the index.

Funding for the project came from the Center for Global Partnership of the Japan Foundation, the Curry Foundation, the Ford Foundation, the Korea Foundation, the Tokyo Club Foundation for Global Studies, the United States–Japan Foundation, and the Alex C. Walker Educational and Charitable Foundation. The author and Brookings are grateful for their support.

The views expressed in this book are those of the author and should not be ascribed to any of the persons or organizations acknowledged above, or to the trustees, officers, or staff members of the Brookings Institution.

BRUCE K. MACLAURY
President

November 1994
Washington, D.C.

Contents

Preface to the Studies on Integrating National Economies

E CONOMIC interdependence among nations has increased sharply in the past half century. For example, while the value of total production of industrial countries increased at a rate of about 9 percent a year on average between 1964 and 1992, the value of the exports of those nations grew at an average rate of 12 percent, and lending and borrowing across national borders through banks surged upward even more rapidly at 23 percent a year. This international economic interdependence has contributed to significantly improved standards of living for most countries. Continuing international economic integration holds out the promise of further benefits. Yet the increasing sensitivity of national economies to events and policies originating abroad creates dilemmas and pitfalls if national policies and international cooperation are poorly managed.

The Brookings Project on Integrating National Economies, of which this study is a component, focuses on the interplay between two fundamental facts about the world at the end of the twentieth century. First, the world will continue for the foreseeable future to be organized politically into nation-states with sovereign governments. Second, increasing economic integration among nations will continue to erode differences among national economies and undermine the autonomy of national governments. The project explores the opportunities and tensions arising from these two facts.

Scholars from a variety of disciplines have produced twenty-one studies for the first phase of the project. Each study examines the heightened competition between national political sovereignty and

increased cross-border economic integration. This preface identi-
fies background themes and issues common to all the studies and
provides a brief overview of the project as a whole.[1]

Increasing World Economic Integration

Two underlying sets of causes have led nations to become more
closely intertwined. First, technological, social, and cultural changes
have sharply reduced the effective economic distances among
nations. Second, many of the government policies that traditionally inhibited cross-border transactions have been relaxed or even
dismantled.

The same improvements in transportation and communications
technology that make it much easier and cheaper for companies in
New York to ship goods to California, for residents of Strasbourg
to visit relatives in Marseilles, and for investors in Hokkaido to buy
and sell shares on the Tokyo Stock Exchange facilitate trade,
migration, and capital movements spanning nations and conti-
nents. The sharply reduced costs of moving goods, money, people,
and information underlie the profound economic truth that technology has made the world markedly smaller.

New communications technology has been especially significant
for financial activity. Computers, switching devices, and telecommunications satellites have slashed the cost of transmitting information internationally, of confirming transactions, and of paying
for transactions. In the 1950s, for example, foreign exchange could
be bought and sold only during conventional business hours in the
initiating party's time zone. Such transactions can now be carried
out instantaneously twenty-four hours a day. Large banks pass the
management of their worldwide foreign-exchange positions
around the globe from one branch to another, staying continu-
ously ahead of the setting sun.

Such technological innovations have increased the knowledge of
potentially profitable international exchanges and of economic opportunities abroad. Those developments, in turn, have changed

---

1. A complete list of authors and study titles is included at the beginning of this volume,
facing the title page.

consumers' and producers' tastes. Foreign goods, foreign vacations, foreign financial investments—virtually anything from other nations—have lost some of their exotic character.

Although technological change permits increased contact among nations, it would not have produced such dramatic effects if it had been countermanded by government policies. Governments have traditionally taxed goods moving in international trade, directly restricted imports and subsidized exports, and tried to limit international capital movements. Those policies erected "separation fences" at the borders of nations. From the perspective of private sector agents, separation fences imposed extra costs on cross-border transactions. They reduced trade and, in some cases, eliminated it. During the 1930s governments used such policies with particular zeal, a practice now believed to have deepened and lengthened the Great Depression.

After World War II, most national governments began—sometimes unilaterally, more often collaboratively—to lower their separation fences, to make them more permeable, or sometimes even to tear down parts of them. The multilateral negotiations under the auspices of the General Agreement on Trade and Tariffs (GATT)—for example, the Kennedy Round in the 1960s, the Tokyo Round in the 1970s, and most recently the protracted negotiations of the Uruguay Round, formally signed only in April 1994—stand out as the most prominent examples of fence lowering for trade in goods. Though contentious and marked by many compromises, the GATT negotiations are responsible for sharp reductions in at-the-border restrictions on trade in goods and services. After the mid-1980s a large number of developing countries moved unilaterally to reduce border barriers and to pursue outwardly oriented policies.

The lowering of fences for financial transactions began later and was less dramatic. Nonetheless, by the 1990s government restrictions on capital flows, especially among the industrial countries, were much less important and widespread than at the end of World War II and in the 1950s.

By shrinking the economic distances among nations, changes in technology would have progressively integrated the world economy even in the absence of reductions in governments' separation fences. Reductions in separation fences would have enhanced interdependence even without the technological innovations. Together, these two sets of evolutionary changes have reinforced each other and strikingly transformed the world economy.

Changes in the Government of Nations

Simultaneously with the transformation of the global economy, major changes have occurred in the world's political structure. First, the number of governmental decisionmaking units in the world has expanded markedly and political power has been diffused more broadly among them. Rising nationalism and, in some areas, heightened ethnic tensions have accompanied that increasing political pluralism.

The history of membership in international organizations documents the sharp growth in the number of independent states. For example, only 44 nations participated in the Bretton Woods conference of July 1944, which gave birth to the International Monetary Fund. But by the end of 1970, the IMF had 118 member nations. The number of members grew to 150 by the mid-1980s and to 178 by December 1993. Much of this growth reflects the collapse of colonial empires. Although many nations today are small and carry little individual weight in the global economy, their combined influence is considerable and their interests cannot be ignored as easily as they were in the past.

A second political trend, less visible but equally important, has been the gradual loss of the political and economic hegemony of the United States. Immediately after World War II, the United States by itself accounted for more than one-third of world production. By the early 1990s the U.S. share had fallen to about one-fifth. Concurrently, the political and economic influence of the European colonial powers continued to wane, and the economic significance of nations outside Europe and North America, such as Japan, Korea, Indonesia, China, Brazil, and Mexico, increased. A world in which economic power and influence are widely diffused has displaced a world in which one or a few nations effectively dominated international decision-making.

Turmoil and the prospect of fundamental change in the formerly centrally planned economies compose a third factor causing radical changes in world politics. During the era of central planning, governments in those nations tried to limit external influences on their economies. Now leaders in the formerly planned economies are trying to adopt reforms modeled on Western capitalist principles. To the extent that these efforts succeed, those nations will increase their economic involvement with the rest of the world. Political and economic alignments among the Western industrialized nations will be forced to adapt.

Governments and scholars have begun to assess these three trends, but their far-reaching ramifications will not be clear for decades.

Dilemmas for National Policies

Cross-border economic integration and national political sovereignty have increasingly come into conflict, leading to a growing mismatch between the economic and political structures of the world. The effective domains of economic markets have come to coincide less and less with national governmental jurisdictions.

When the separation fences at nations' borders were high, governments and citizens could sharply distinguish "international" from "domestic" policies. International policies dealt with at-the-border barriers, such as tariffs and quotas, or responded to events occurring abroad. In contrast, domestic policies were concerned with everything behind the nation's borders, such as competition and antitrust rules, corporate governance, product standards, worker safety, regulation and supervision of financial institutions, environmental protection, tax codes, and the government's budget. Domestic policies were regarded as matters about which nations were sovereign, to be determined by the preferences of the nation's citizens and its political institutions, without regard for effects on other nations.

As separation fences have been lowered and technological innovations have shrunk economic distances, a multitude of formerly ne-

glected differences among nations' domestic policies have become
exposed to international scrutiny. National governments and international negotiations must thus increasingly deal with "deeper"—
behind-the-border—integration. For example, if country A permits
companies to emit air and water pollutants whereas country B does
not, companies that use pollution-generating methods of production
will find it cheaper to produce in country A. Companies in country B
that compete internationally with companies in country A are likely
to complain that foreign competitors enjoy unfair advantages and to
press for international pollution standards.

Deeper integration requires analysis of the economic and the
political aspects of virtually all nonborder policies and practices.
Such issues have already figured prominently in negotiations over
the evolution of the European Community, over the Uruguay
Round of GATT negotiations, over the North American Free
Trade Agreement (NAFTA), and over the bilateral economic relationships between Japan and the United States. Future debates
about behind-the-border policies will occur with increasing frequency and prove at least as complex and contentious as the past
negotiations regarding at-the-border restrictions.

Tensions about deeper integration arise from three broad sources:
cross-border spillovers, diminished national autonomy, and challenges to political sovereignty.

Cross-Border Spillovers

Some activities in one nation produce consequences that spill
across borders and affect other nations. Illustrations of these spillovers abound. Given the impact of modern technology of banking
and securities markets in creating interconnected networks, lax
rules in one nation erode the ability of all other nations to enforce
banking and securities rules and to deal with fraudulent transactions. Given the rapid diffusion of knowledge, science and technology policies in one nation generate knowledge that other nations
can use without full payment. Labor market policies become matters of concern to other nations because workers migrate in search
of work; policies in one nation can trigger migration that floods or
starves labor markets elsewhere. When one nation dumps pollu-

tants into the air or water that other nations breathe or drink, the matter goes beyond the unitary concern of the polluting nation and becomes a matter for international negotiation. Indeed, the hydrocarbons that are emitted into the atmosphere when individual nations burn coal for generating electricity contribute to global warming and are thereby a matter of concern for the entire world.

The tensions associated with cross-border spillovers can be especially vexing when national policies generate outcomes alleged to be competitively inequitable, as in the example in which country A permits companies to emit pollutants and country B does not. Or consider a situation in which country C requires commodities, whether produced at home or abroad, to meet certain design standards, justified for safety reasons. Foreign competitors may find it too expensive to meet these standards. In that event, the standards in C act very much like tariffs or quotas, effectively narrowing or even eliminating foreign competition for domestic producers. Citing examples of this sort, producers or governments in individual nations often complain that business is not conducted on a "level playing field." Typically, the complaining nation proposes that *other* nations adjust their policies to moderate or remove the competitive inequities.

Arguments for creating a level playing field are troublesome at best. International trade occurs precisely because of differences among nations—in resource endowments, labor skills, and consumer tastes. Nations specialize in producing goods and services in which they are relatively most efficient. In a fundamental sense, cross-border trade is valuable because the playing field is *not* level.

When David Ricardo first developed the theory of comparative advantage, he focused on differences among nations owing to climate or technology. But Ricardo could as easily have ascribed the productive differences to differing "social climates" as to physical or technological climates. Taking all "climatic" differences as given, the theory of comparative advantage argues that free trade among nations will maximize global welfare.

Taken to its logical extreme, the notion of leveling the playing field implies that nations should become homogeneous in all major respects. But that recommendation is unrealistic and even pernicious. Suppose country A decides that it is too poor to afford the costs of a clean environment, and will thus permit the production of goods that pollute local air and water supplies. Or suppose it concludes that it cannot afford stringent protections for worker safety. Country A will then argue that it is inappropriate for other nations to impute to country A the value they themselves place on a clean environment and safety standards (just as it would be inappropriate to impute the A valuations to the environment of other nations). The core of the idea of political sovereignty is to permit national residents to order their lives and property in accord with their own preferences.

Which perspective about differences among nations in behind-the-border policies is more compelling? Is country A merely exercising its national preferences and appropriately exploiting its comparative advantage in goods that are dirty or dangerous to produce? Or does a legitimate international problem exist that justifies pressure from other nations urging country A to accept changes in its policies (thus curbing its national sovereignty)? When national governments negotiate resolutions to such questions—trying to agree whether individual nations are legitimately exercising sovereign choices or, alternatively, engaging in behavior that is unfair or damaging to other nations—the dialogue is invariably contentious because the resolutions depend on the typically complex circumstances of the international spillovers and on the relative weights accorded to the interests of particular individuals and particular nations.

Diminished National Autonomy

As cross-border economic integration increases, governments experience greater difficulties in trying to control events within their borders. Those difficulties, summarized by the term *diminished autonomy*, are the second set of reasons why tensions arise from the competition between political sovereignty and economic integration.

For example, nations adjust monetary and fiscal policies to influence domestic inflation and employment. In setting these policies, smaller countries have always been somewhat constrained by foreign economic events and policies. Today, however, all nations are constrained, often severely. More than in the past, therefore, nations may be better able to achieve their economic goals if they work together collaboratively in adjusting their macroeconomic policies.

Diminished autonomy and cross-border spillovers can sometimes be allowed to persist without explicit international cooperation to deal with them. States in the United States adopt their own tax systems and set policies for assistance to poor single people without any formal cooperation or limitation. Market pressures operate to force a degree of de facto cooperation. If one state taxes corporations too heavily, it knows business will move elsewhere. (Those familiar with older debates about "fiscal federalism" within the United States and other nations will recognize the similarity between those issues and the emerging international debates about deeper integration of national economies.) Analogously, differences among nations in regulations, standards, policies, institutions, and even social and cultural preferences create economic incentives for a kind of arbitrage that erodes or eliminates the differences. Such pressures involve not only the conventional arbitrage that exploits price differentials (buying at one point in geographic space or time and selling at another) but also shifts in the location of production facilities and in the residence of factors of production.

In many other cases, however, cross-border spillovers, arbitrage pressures, and diminished effectiveness of national policies can produce unwanted consequences. In cases involving what economists call externalities (external economies and diseconomies), national governments may need to cooperate to promote mutual interests. For example, population growth, continued urbanization, and the more intensive exploitation of natural resources generate external diseconomies not only within but across national boundaries. External economies generated when benefits spill across national jurisdictions probably also increase in importance (for instance, the gains from basic research and from control of communicable diseases).

None of these situations is new, but technological change and the reduction of tariffs and quotas heighten their importance. When one nation produces goods (such as scientific research) or "bads" (such as pollution) that significantly affect other nations, individual governments acting sequentially and noncooperatively cannot deal effectively with the resulting issues. In the absence of explicit cooperation and political leadership, too few collective goods and too many collective bads will be supplied.

Challenges to Political Sovereignty

The pressures from cross-border economic integration sometimes even lead individuals or governments to challenge the core assumptions of national political sovereignty. Such challenges are a third source of tensions about deeper integration.

The existing world system of nation-states assumes that a nation's residents are free to follow their own values and to select their own political arrangements without interference from others. Similarly, property rights are allocated by nation. (The so-called global commons, such as outer space and the deep seabed, are the sole exceptions.) A nation is assumed to have the sovereign right to exploit its property in accordance with its own preferences and policies. Political sovereignty is thus analogous to the concept of consumer sovereignty (the presumption that the individual consumer best knows his or her own interests and should exercise them freely).

In times of war, some nations have had sovereignty wrested from them by force. In earlier eras, a handful of individuals or groups have questioned the premises of political sovereignty. With the profound increases in economic integration in recent decades, however, a larger number of individuals and groups—and occasionally even their national governments—have identified circumstances in which, it is claimed, some universal or international set of values should take precedence over the preferences or policies of particular nations.

Some groups seize on human-rights issues, for example, or what they deem to be egregiously inappropriate political arrangements in other nations. An especially prominent case occurred when citizens in many nations labeled the former apartheid policies of South Africa an affront to universal values and emphasized that the South African government was not legitimately representing the interests of a majority of South Africa's residents. Such views caused many national governments to apply economic sanctions against South Africa. Examples of value conflicts are not restricted to human rights, however. Groups focusing on environmental issues characterize tropical rain forests as the lungs of the world and the genetic repository for numerous species of plants and animals that are the heritage of all mankind. Such views lead Europeans, North Americans, or Japanese to challenge the timber-cutting policies of Brazilians and Indonesians. A recent controversy over tuna fishing with long drift nets that kill porpoises is yet another example. Environmentalists in the United States whose sensibilities were offended by the drowning of porpoises required U.S. boats at some additional expense to amend their fishing practices. The U.S. fishermen, complaining about imported tuna caught with less regard for porpoises, persuaded the U.S. government to ban such tuna imports (both direct imports from the countries in which the tuna is caught and indirect imports shipped via third countries). Mexico and Venezuela were the main countries affected by this ban; a GATT dispute panel sided with Mexico against the United States in the controversy, which further upset the U.S. environmental community.

A common feature of all such examples is the existence, real or alleged, of "psychological externalities" or "political failures." Those holding such views reject untrammeled political sovereignty for nation-states in deference to universal or non-national values. They wish to constrain the exercise of individual nations' sovereignties through international negotiations or, if necessary, by even stronger intervention.

The Management of International Convergence

In areas in which arbitrage pressures and cross-border spillovers are weak and psychological or political externalities are largely absent, national governments may encounter few problems with deeper integration. Diversity across nations may persist quite easily. But at the other extreme, arbitrage and spillovers in some areas may be so strong that they threaten to erode national diversity completely. Or psychological and political sensitivities may be asserted too powerfully to be ignored. Governments will then be confronted with serious tensions, and national policies and behaviors may eventually converge to common, worldwide patterns (for example, subject to internationally agreed norms or minimum standards). Eventual convergence across nations, if it occurs, could happen in a harmful way (national policies and practices being driven to a least common denominator with externalities ignored, in effect a "race to the bottom") or it could occur with mutually beneficial results ("survival of the fittest and the best").

Each study in this series addresses basic questions about the management of international convergence: if, when, and how national governments should intervene to try to influence the consequences of arbitrage pressures, cross-border spillovers, diminished autonomy, and the assertion of psychological or political externalities. A wide variety of responses is conceivable. We identify six, which should be regarded not as distinct categories but as ranges along a continuum.

National autonomy defines a situation at one end of the continuum in which national governments make decentralized decisions with little or no consultation and no explicit cooperation. This response represents political sovereignty at its strongest, undiluted by any international management of convergence.

Mutual recognition, like national autonomy, presumes decentralized decisions by national governments and relies on market competition to guide the process of international convergence. Mutual recognition, however, entails exchanges of information and consultations among governments to constrain the formation of national regulations and policies. As understood in discussions of economic integration within the European Community, moreover, mutual recognition entails an explicit acceptance by each member nation of the regulations, standards, and certification procedures of other members. For example, mutual recognition allows wine or liquor produced in any European Union country to be sold in all twelve member countries even if production standards in member countries differ. Doctors licensed in France are permitted to practice in

Germany, and vice versa, even if licensing procedures in the two countries differ.

Governments may agree on rules that restrict their freedom to set policy or that promote gradual convergence in the structure of policy. As international consultations and monitoring of compliance with such rules become more important, this situation can be described as *monitored decentralization*. The Group of Seven finance ministers meetings, supplemented by the IMF's surveillance over exchange rate and macroeconomic policies, illustrate this approach to management.

Coordination goes further than mutual recognition and monitored decentralization in acknowledging convergence pressures. It is also more ambitious in promoting intergovernmental cooperation to deal with them. Coordination involves jointly designed mutual adjustments of national policies. In clear-cut cases of coordination, bargaining occurs and governments agree to behave differently from the ways they would have behaved without the agreement. Examples include the World Health Organization's procedures for controlling communicable diseases and the 1987 Montreal Protocol (to a 1985 framework convention) for the protection of stratospheric ozone by reducing emissions of chlorofluorocarbons.

Explicit harmonization, which requires still higher levels of intergovernmental cooperation, may require agreement on regional standards or world standards. Explicit harmonization typically entails still greater departures from decentralization in decisionmaking and still further strengthening of international institutions. The 1988 agreement among major central banks to set minimum standards for the required capital positions of commercial banks (reached through the Committee on Banking Regulations and Supervisory Practices at the Bank for International Settlements) is an example of partially harmonized regulations.

At the opposite end of the spectrum from national autonomy lies *federalist mutual governance*, which implies continuous bargaining and joint, centralized decisionmaking. To make federalist mutual governance work would require greatly strengthened supranational institutions. This end of the management spectrum,

now relevant only as an analytical benchmark, is a possible outcome that can be imagined for the middle or late decades of the
twenty-first century, possibly even sooner for regional groupings
like the European Union.

Overview of the Brookings Project

Despite their growing importance, the issues of deeper economic integration and its competition with national political sovereignty were largely neglected in the 1980s. In 1992 the Brookings
Institution initiated its project on Integrating National Economies
to direct attention to these important questions.

In studying this topic, Brookings sought and received the cooperation of some of the world's leading economists, political
scientists, foreign-policy specialists, and government officials, representing all regions of the world. Although some functional areas
require a special focus on European, Japanese, and North American perspectives, at all junctures the goal was to include, in
addition, the perspectives of developing nations and the formerly
centrally planned economies.

The first phase of the project commissioned the twenty-one
scholarly studies listed at the beginning of the book. One or two
lead discussants, typically residents of parts of the world other than
the area where the author resides, were asked to comment on each
study.

Authors enjoyed substantial freedom to design their individual
studies, taking due account of the overall themes and goals of the
project. The guidelines for the studies requested that at least some
of the analysis be carried out with a non-normative perspective. In
effect, authors were asked to develop a "baseline" of what might
happen in the absence of changed policies or further international
cooperation. For their normative analyses, authors were asked to
start with an agnostic posture that did not prejudge the net benefits or costs resulting from integration. The project organizers
themselves had no presumption about whether national diversity is
better or worse than international convergence or about what the
individual studies should conclude regarding the desirability of

increased integration. On the contrary, each author was asked to address the trade-offs in his or her issue area between diversity and convergence and to locate the area, currently and prospectively, on the spectrum of international management possibilities running between national autonomy through mutual recognition to coordination and explicit harmonization.

HENRY J. AARON   SUSAN M. COLLINS
RALPH C. BRYANT   ROBERT Z. LAWRENCE

Chapter 1

Introduction

*H*AVING WON the cold war, the United States is suddenly without a familiar role to play beyond its own borders, and lacking such a role it faces a strong temptation to turn inward.[1] What would such an inward turn mean for U.S. leadership in the world economy? And why is such leadership important?

History shows that whenever large and influential states have taken a lead in embracing open economic policies, the world economy has been able to move toward deeper integration and grow more quickly. When leading states have not embraced such policies, deeper integration has been more difficult to attain. This pattern developed in the mid-nineteenth century when Great Britain provided market-opening leadership with its unilateral repeal of the Corn Laws in 1846. Other European nations then embraced liberal trade as well, and between 1840 and 1870 international trade more than quadrupled.[2] When Britain's relative strength subsequently declined, and its free trade leadership finally collapsed early in the 1930s, open borders were supplanted by high tariffs and separate currency blocs. Between 1928 and 1935 world

---

1. President Clinton reflected on this temptation in a 1994 CNN broadcast to more than 200 countries and territories around the world: "With the cold war over," he said, "there are pressures here in America, as elsewhere, to turn inward, to focus on needs here at home." Gwen Ifill, "Clinton Defends . . . Record," *New York Times,* May 4, 1994, p. A12.
2. See Rogowski (1989). Not all analysts attribute such importance to Britain's leadership, especially after 1870. See Murphy (1994).

trade fell by 65 percent, a reversal of international economic integration that deepened the Great Depression.[3]

After World War II, policy leadership by the United States helped to reopen the world economy. Responding in large part to cold war security concerns, the U.S. government provided generous Marshall Plan assistance to revive war-shattered European economies and offered the dollar as a key currency to restabilize the international monetary system. Private U.S. business firms spread their superior technologies and management skills abroad through direct foreign investment, and competing foreign firms were granted generous trade access to the large and lucrative U.S. domestic market. Between 1948 and 1980, partly as a result of U.S. leadership, the volume of world trade increased at an average annual rate of 6.7 percent, doubling roughly every eleven years; economic integration deepened as never before. Among the industrial nations of the Organization for Economic Cooperation and Development (OECD), the average ratio of trade to GDP nearly doubled between 1960 and 1980, increasing to 41.4 percent.[4]

Thanks to U.S. leadership, peace among the western industrial countries was guaranteed along with prosperity. West Germany and Japan were transformed from dissatisfied predators into pacified democracies capable of resisting the intimidation of Soviet communism. With U.S. support, the states of western Europe began moving toward various forms of regionwide economic and political integration.

Although these spectacular postwar gains were made possible in part by U.S. leadership, the gains have now grown so complete, especially with the defeat of Soviet communism, as to undermine the foundation on which U.S. leadership initiatives were built. There is no longer a cold war security imperative to inspire generous economic policy leadership from the United States or to ensure that the rival market economies in Europe and Japan will follow the U.S. lead. So successful was the United States in promoting the prosperity of rival market economies during the cold war that the unchallenged financial and technological supremacy

3. See Rogowski (1989, pp. 21, 62).
4. Rogowski (1989, p. 88).

of the United States, which once created further incentives and opportunities for U.S. leadership, is now also diminished.

It is assumed in this book that the world economy still requires effective policy leadership, if only because of the adjustment strains generated by today's rapid pace of technological change. The question is whether international leadership will be jeopardized if the United States should turn its economic attentions inward in a post–cold war mood of withdrawal and self-absorption. In this book I argue that giving first attention to internal policy within the United States may not be bad for the world economy, and that in today's circumstances effective U.S. international leadership may have to begin at home.

Chapter 2

Outward-First and Inward-First Leadership

WHAT has been called foreign economic policy is now usually as much domestic as it is foreign. The international and domestic components of foreign economic policy are so intermingled that some analysts have sought to label such issues "intermestic."[1] It is the intermingling of these traditionally distinct policy realms that is the concern of this book. When dealing with an issue that is both foreign and domestic at the same time, policymakers often face a practical choice of where to begin—at home or abroad.

A narrow but politically realistic interpretation of U.S. policy goals is assumed here: U.S. policymakers should pursue the national economic interest, however difficult that may be to define. Economists seeking to maximize efficient resource use worldwide may not like such a nationalized definition of interests; even some political scientists have argued for a cosmopolitan set of "world interest" goals.[2] But for the immediate future it can be assumed that a narrow national interest policy will remain politically essential.

A key choice is thus where to begin pursuit of the national economic interest. When policy realms intermingle, leadership action can be launched either at home or abroad. To illustrate in

1. See Manning (1977).
2. See Brown (1988, p. 307).

4

the area of macroeconomic policy, an outward-first starting point might be an international cooperation and surveillance agreement, negotiated and then managed through the Group of Seven (G-7); an inward-first starting point might be tougher unilateral action on fiscal imbalances at home. The distinction between these approaches is based more on sequences of action than on policy substance. With either approach the final goal could be the same (for example, improved U.S. fiscal policy discipline and international macroeconomic policy coordination); either starting point could produce the same set of final policy actions. A G-7 agreement might be intended to lead to tougher budget actions at home (an outside-to-inside approach), just as unilateral budget discipline at home might be intended to lay the groundwork for improved international cooperation agreements within the G-7 (an inside-to-outside approach).

Sequencing is important because it helps to broaden or narrow the range of policy options that are politically available. Policy initiatives usually run into a range of opposition, both ideological and self-interested, at home and abroad; whatever success they achieve in one arena can influence their prospects for success in the other. In this sense, policy success is path-dependent. Several paths of sequence may exist to the same policy goal, but in practical political terms some paths may be more inviting than others.

Leadership in international economic policy must therefore be appreciated as a two-level game, in which the politics of negotiation abroad (the international game) cannot be separated from the politics of ratification at home (the domestic game), and in which prior actions go a long way toward determining the subsequent range of options that are politically available. Robert D. Putnam, who has done the most to advance formal understanding of the links between international agreement and domestic ratification, has shown that political leaders can either gain or lose bargaining advantages in these simultaneous games, depending on their management of the interface between the two.[3]

3. Putnam (1988).

Outward-First Leadership

U.S. foreign economic policymakers have traditionally been attracted to the outward-first approach, partly because it tends to solidify their institutional jurisdiction over policymaking processes (especially if the starting point involves an official negotiation with foreign governments) and partly because it may offer a useful tactic for weakening or isolating domestic policy opposition. As an example, the launching of an international trade negotiation can be used as a means to preempt protectionist demands that might otherwise arise and prevail at home.

Robert Putnam is careful to maintain that in a successful two-level bargaining process either an internal or an external initiative could be taken first. Yet his own examples reflect a clear outward-first orientation. His favorite example is the agreement on macro-economic stimulation and energy policy reached by the heads of government of West Germany, Japan, and the United States at the Bonn economic summit in 1978.[4] In this agreement, Chancellor Helmut Schmidt agreed to an added fiscal stimulus in West Germany, Prime Minister Takeo Fukuda agreed to seek higher Japanese growth rates, and President Jimmy Carter committed the United States to decontrolling domestic crude oil prices within two years. This public exchange of commitments on the world stage strengthened the hand of each leader in subsequent policy battles at home, enabling each to implement the commitments made. The nonenergy part of the Bonn agreement was later challenged on substantive grounds because inflation was aggravated and a severe recession followed in 1980–81.[5] Nevertheless, the 1978 summit reveals the attraction of the outward-first approach to foreign economic policy officials facing domestic political constraints.

Some risks associated with the outward-first approach must be carefully considered. When governments initiate policies abroad before they have secured a consensus for such policies at home,

---

4. Putnam (1988, pp. 428–29).

5. The problem, according to Wendy Dobson, was "the poor timing of the agreed-upon policies, together with the totally unexpected oil shock that intervened in 1979." Dobson (1991, p. 15).

they damage their international reputation if the intended domestic consensus subsequently fails to emerge. Thirty years ago Henry Kissinger warned against using international negotiations as a means to "make up our own mind" at home.[6]

Outward-first initiatives may also make the emergence of a domestic consensus more difficult. Once an international negotiation has been launched, agreement on policy reforms at home may be viewed, in the context of the negotiation, as a price paid to secure cooperation from foreigners. The difficult issue of appropriate international burden-sharing may also be raised and become a sticking point. Because opposition politicians at home may find it easy to characterize foreigners as never doing enough, raising the burden-sharing issue can strengthen the hand of opposition politicians.

By opening opportunities for politicians to criticize foreigners, the outward-first approach can diminish overall political accountability, both within governments and among governments. This is perhaps the greatest danger of all. What little political accountability there is in today's world economy tends to be found within the borders of democratic nations with elected officials. Until the day when foreigners can cast votes across borders, accountability will best be preserved if officials act first within their own borders. Opportunistic leaders may otherwise be tempted to make unreasonable outward-first demands on foreigners, who do not vote, in order to mask their own policy failings at home. If the policy sins of foreigners (trade restrictions, environmental failings, weak labor protection) are allowed to dominate debate at home, the discipline to correct failings at home can be lost.

Inward-First Leadership

The inward-first approach to economic policy leadership has seldom been examined carefully on its own terms. Few policy analysts have wished to advocate inward-first actions. In part this attitude reflects the success of so many outward-first initiatives by

6. See Kissinger (1965, p. 158).

the United States during the early postwar era, yet it also reflects a justified wariness in the United States toward any policy that might seem protectionist, unilateralist, or isolationist.

Because inward-first action is defined here in terms of policy sequence rather than policy content, any association with protectionism would be unfair. Actions taken at home first can just as well be liberal as protectionist (such as a unilateral lowering of domestic farm subsidies). If well considered, inward-first policy actions can even be the best guarantee against demands by domestic industry for unilateral trade protection (for example, internal fiscal and monetary policies that keep long-term interest rates low enough to prevent a sudden currency appreciation that would trigger industry demands for protection). Inward-first actions are not necessarily protectionist any more than outward-first actions are necessarily liberal. Statists who see cross-border flows of money, goods, technology, and people as things that governments must collectively manage in an outward-first manner, are hardly offering a liberal vision.

Invidious associations with unilateralism are also unfair. Acting at home first does not preclude subsequent multilateral cooperation abroad. Prior unilateral actions can actually be the surest means for a leading nation to promote multilateral cooperation. In the examination of macroeconomic policy coordination, agricultural policy reform, and global environmental policy in chapter 5, it will be seen that successful international cooperation has often required prior unilateral domestic policy actions by the United States.

In the 1930s unilateralism was protectionist and noncooperative, but a longer view of history reveals that unilateral trade policy actions by leading states—if liberal, rather than illiberal—can sometimes widen the path toward multilateral agreements and deeper multilateral market integration. As discussed earlier, Great Britain's unilateral repeal of the Corn Laws in 1846 led to a subsequent era of internationally negotiated trade liberalization. Britain's internal market was so large that a unilateral embrace of free trade in agriculture was enough to send strong signals of commercial opportunity, through private commodity markets, to other political actors worldwide. This indirectly facilitated the emergence of political coalitions favoring free trade policies in other nations. Scott C. James and David A. Lake have described this indirect form of international leadership as a "second face of hegemony."[7] Great Britain also used more visible outward-looking means (the "first face" of its hegemony) in subsequent years to negotiate international free-trade agreements; James and Lake argue that the foundation for this more conventional exercise in leadership was a bold unilateral action taken without prior commitments of reciprocity from abroad.[8]

Britain's unilateral liberalizing action was taken at the border rather than behind the border, so technically it cannot be counted as an inward-first step. Yet it shows that international negotiations among governments are not the only way to initiate cooperative policy convergence among states. Britain used international market forces to encourage policy convergence, then negotiated later. Market channels are in some ways even more effective than diplomatic channels in communicating to foreign governments examples of what a sound policy should look like. The rapid growth of cross-border private sector activity does not have to be seen as a constraint on leadership options, or as a threat to political control that requires intergovernmental management. Leading nations that unilaterally undertake liberal economic policy actions— either internally, at the border, or beyond—can trigger international private sector reactions that in turn encourage comparably liberal policy actions by foreign governments.

As for the demon of isolationism, it is more of an issue for diplomatic and security policy than for economic policy. Even George Washington, the original advocate of a disengaged diplomatic and security posture for the United States, sought at all times to promote U.S. commerce abroad.

The most articulate advocate of examining inward-first leadership options on their own terms has been Henry R. Nau of George

---

7. See James and Lake (1989).

8. As James and Lake (1989) explain, "From the hegemon's perspective, the beauty of the second face lies in its subtlety; its aims are realized through the 'invisible hand' of international market power. Once set in motion by its own policy initiatives, say by lowering tariffs, the process is automatic and hidden from view by the veil of market forces. The exercise of power, however, is nonetheless real" (p. 8).

Washington University. Like Putnam, Nau appreciates the complex dynamic of two-level game policy interactions. Nau has suggested that rather than playing this game through outward-first internationalism an alternative approach should be used, which he has called domesticism. By domesticism Nau means the vigorous use of national action at home and in the private marketplace to create market conditions that would enable and encourage other governments to follow suit.[9]

To justify this unilateral approach, Nau argues that policy processes (such as cooperation) are less important than policy content,[10] and that correcting bad policy is more important than policy harmonization. Nau advocates policies that would move the world economy toward low inflation, strong market incentives, and open borders; these goals could best be reached through U.S. initiatives that begin at home rather than abroad.

Nau's deference to private markets makes him skeptical of allowing governments to use traditional outward-first techniques to "manage interdependence." He fears it would be too easy for opportunistic politicians to use such techniques to escape both political and market disciplines. He prefers international policy convergence built around the known disciplines of market competition rather than around the more suspect or elusive disciplines of international deal-making among domestically elected politicians.[11]

Nau's approach places heavy reliance on market-based policy coordination mechanisms, but he does not rule out the use of international institutions or the pursuit of government-to-government agreements.[12] Nau states a preference for what he calls a "soft" international institutional approach, especially in areas such as macroeconomic coordination and exchange rate stability. I believe that inward-first advocates need not be quite this strict; policy initiatives first taken at home could be designed to pave the way for "hard" as well as "soft" intergovernmental agreements.

9. Nau (1985, p. 16) For a closer look at Nau's argument, including his response to criticism from C. Fred Bergsten, see Bergsten and Nau (1985).

10. Nau (1985).

11. See Nau (1990, pp. 348–49).

12. To Nau's credit, he makes explicit room for nonmarket management tools. His critics, who stress such tools, seldom make explicit room for market mechanisms.

Some might challenge the inward-first approach on the grounds that it favors a narrow definition of the national interest, one that imposes negative externalities or negative cross-border spillovers on nations abroad. An inward-looking U.S. macroeconomic policy, for example, could produce unwanted inflationary or deflationary effects abroad; inward-looking farm price support policies could destabilize international commodity markets; and domestic energy tax and price policies, if undertaken with only internal concerns in mind, might result in heedless pollution of the global commons. Even large powers such as the United States have an interest in avoiding the imposition of negative spillovers on others, because a chain of unanticipated or hostile international policy reactions could be generated. In this view the best way to prevent negative spillovers presumably would be to abandon the inward-first approach and incorporate outward-looking international goals into the policymaking process at the start.

These are legitimate concerns. Governments that act first at home are likely to operate from a more restricted (mostly internal) information base, compared with governments that decide to act first abroad. On the other hand, policy success in the smaller and more familiar domestic arena may actually require less information. Governments taking the outward-first approach must accurately judge likely political and commercial reactions to their initiatives abroad as well as at home. Such judgments are difficult to make even in the best of circumstances. Putnam, for example, concedes that even at the Bonn summit in 1978 the international negotiators "were usually wrong in their assessments of domestic politics abroad."[13]

Moreover, as long as inward-first policymakers are paying attention to private markets, which today are deeply integrated across borders, they will automatically have access to quite a bit of global information. Officials in states that have relatively open borders (such as the United States) can learn about international market conditions even when looking within, and may be better informed about available options for successful international action than outward-looking officials, who may spend too

13. Putnam (1988, p. 452).

much time focused on the governmental actions of their foreign counterparts.

Actions taken abroad first are not always more generous than actions taken at home first. Outward-first actions can be self-serving or hostile, as demonstrated in cases of competitive currency devaluations, economic sanctions, negotiated protection, and tit-for-tat subsidy competition. Outward-looking commercial and geopolitical rivalries drove the beggar-thy-neighbor policies of economic nationalism that did such damage to the industrial west during the 1930s and 1940s. Fortunately such economic nationalism is no longer the salient feature it once was among western industrial states, its foundations having been weakened by a dramatic spread of multinational business and investment, which has made national labeling of global production and trade more difficult.[14] Still, the temptation to blame foreigners for domestic economic difficulties could always revive, especially in an era of diminishing threats to common security. Leaders taking an outward-first approach might then become more prone to do damage abroad than leaders taking an inward-first approach.

Although some critics might fault the inward-first approach for not being generous enough to foreigners, other critics could fault it for being too generous. In this view unilateral U.S. policy actions at home, if taken without prior international agreements on equitable burden-sharing, might inadvertently be too generous to foreign governments by giving those governments unintended opportunities to take a free ride. If the United States were to act unilaterally in a naive belief that others would be inspired to follow the lead, perhaps it would find itself acting alone. Thus if the United States unilaterally sets environmental standards higher than those of its neighbors, the neighbors might be tempted to retain their lower standards to attract more international investment. If the United States unilaterally reforms its domestic agricultural support policies, the result might be higher international market prices and therefore less pressure on foreign rivals to reform. If the United States tries to reduce its budget deficit unilaterally at home, without first securing a promise that other

14. See Reich (1992).

leading governments would provide some offsetting fiscal stimulus, the U.S. economy could be left alone among the major powers bearing the full burden of adjustment. Unilateral domestic action, according to this view, would probably offer too many positive spillovers abroad.

It is thus hard to criticize the inward-first approach on grounds of generosity alone, because its critics cannot agree on whether it would be too generous to foreign governments or not generous enough. The choice between an inward-first and an outward-first approach depends on more than abstract logic. It also depends on changing historical circumstances, and on the distinctiveness of U.S. political institutions and processes. These interacting concerns are discussed in the next chapters.

Chapter 3

Changing Circumstances

THROUGHOUT most of the exceptional forty-year period that followed World War II, U.S. government officials maintained a record of strong leadership on the basis of outward-first policies. The outward-first approach worked so well that most analysts stopped considering the alternative.

A first step toward reviewing leadership options for the United States in the decades ahead must be recognition that the post–World War II era has now decisively passed. As Jeffrey E. Garten has argued, U.S. officials may find this psychologically difficult: "Part of America's outdated self-image is still related to the memory of the Pax Americana, the era of omnipotence for the twenty years following World War II. . . . These were very special years in the American experience, to be fondly remembered, even cherished. But they were, looking back, a transition period. . . . We need to find a way to put these years and what they represent behind us."[1]

It is essential to recall how exceptional the post–World War II period was in the longer history of the nation and in the longer history of U.S. relations with other nations. The outward-looking internationalism that dominated U.S. policymaking after World War II was a striking departure from historical tradition.

1. Garten (1992, p. 225). In 1993 Jeffrey Garten became the U.S. Commerce Department's undersecretary for international trade.

George Washington, who helped set that tradition in his 1796 Farewell Address, advised his countrymen to capitalize on their "detached and distant situation" from Europe by avoiding permanent diplomatic alliances.[2] This position was elaborated in the Monroe Doctrine in 1823, which specified that Europe and America should essentially keep out of one another's hemispheres. As the relative power of the United States increased with westward expansion and successful industrialization, temptation arose to abandon this inward-looking tradition, yet the foundation for an alternative approach never proved durable. During the McKinley and Theodore Roosevelt administrations, the United States did extend its foreign policy activities beyond the Western Hemisphere and into the Pacific, but not to Europe. In 1916 President Wilson ran a successful reelection campaign on the proud claim to have kept his country out of the disastrous European war, and when he subsequently took the United States into that war and tried to follow up military victory with an explicitly outward-looking collective security policy built around the new League of Nations, he was defeated by partisan opponents in the U.S. Senate.

Inward-looking diplomatic neutrality beyond the Western Hemisphere and parts of the Pacific thereafter reemerged as a U.S. foreign policy norm. In the 1930s Congress passed three separate neutrality acts, which legally blocked any U.S. inclination to take sides in the military or diplomatic disputes of Europe and Asia.

This did not imply isolation from international commercial affairs, but U.S. industrial firms remained largely content with protection, having earlier come of age at a time when the domestic market was large enough and growing rapidly enough to make a certain amount of trade protection and corporate parochialism affordable.

Protectionism was not discredited until the period of the Great Depression, following the effects of the Smoot-Hawley Tariff Act of 1930. Only then was President Franklin Roosevelt's State Department able to begin seeking reciprocal tariff reduction agreements abroad. Yet even this tentative embrace of an outward-first

2. Washington described Europe as having interests with only "a very remote relation" to those of the United States. See Kaufman (1969, p. 27).

trade liberalization stance was weakened for more than a decade by industry doubts and partisan opposition.

The Unusual Postwar Period

World War II production demands brought the U.S. economy out of depression and strengthened its technological superiority at a time when rival economies in Europe were being exhausted and destroyed, giving the United States an unprecedented position of economic and military preponderance at war's end. Economically, the U.S. GNP increased by 50 percent in real terms during the war, while the economies of Western Europe shrank overall by 25 percent. Even five years after the war ended, in 1950, the U.S. economy was still three times as large as that of the Soviet Union and ten times that of Japan.[3] U.S. occupying armies dominated political reconstruction in both West Germany and Japan, and across both the Atlantic and the Pacific, U.S. naval and air forces reigned supreme.

Unsure at first of how to use this (partly unsought) global supremacy, the U.S. government for a time placed faith in the independent operation of global multilateral institutions, such as the Security Council of the newly created United Nations, the International Monetary Fund (IMF), the World Bank (IBRD), and a hoped-for International Trade Organization (ITO). In the face of growing demands for U.S. leadership such Wilsonian tendencies eventually gave way. Repeated Soviet vetoes paralyzed the UN Security Council, and the underfinanced IMF and IBRD proved incapable of providing adequate international liquidity to ensure recovery and growth. Accordingly, after the difficult winter of 1946–47, the United States stepped in with unilateral military and economic policy initiatives, most conspicuously the Truman Doctrine and the Marshall Plan.

The outward-first leadership embraced by the United States after 1947 was successful in part because of its remarkable generosity. Beginning with outright grants of economic aid provided

---

3. See Nye (1990, p. 70).

under the Marshall Plan, the international economic terms of peace offered by the United States were unusually openhanded.[4] To allies and defeated adversaries alike, the United States offered economic advantages such as grants, technical assistance, credits, and market access, without demanding perfect reciprocity or immediate repayment. A combination of economic and military security motives lay behind this generous leadership.

In the economic realm, because of its temporary preponderance, the United States could afford to be openhanded. Offering the U.S. dollar to supplement gold as an international key currency and as a new source of much-needed international liquidity implied no great burden at the time, given the large U.S. trade surplus and the massive size of U.S. gold reserves. Offering unprecedented grant aid to Europe was likewise affordable, in part because the U.S. federal budget was not yet under the strain of massive domestic social entitlement programs. Also, the much larger relative size of the U.S. economy meant there was not much difference between doing favors for the world economy as a whole and doing favors directly for the United States. The United States had strong reason to provide public goods such as liquidity, open markets, and currency stability for the world economy because it was for the moment in a position to capture a lion's share of the benefit from those public goods itself. North America in 1947 accounted for 36 percent of world exports, roughly twice its share just before the war in 1937.[5] The United States could lead without yet having to share the fruits of its leadership with fully recovered, highly competitive European or Asian industrial rivals.

It is unlikely that either the U.S. Congress or the American people would have tolerated the openhanded quality of U.S. external economic policy in Europe and the Pacific after 1947 were it not for the perceived urgency of Stalinist (and later Maoist) security threats. C. Fred Bergsten has argued that "most U.S. global economic initiatives, especially those attempting to create systematic structures in the early postwar years, were primarily motivated by security concerns."[6] Large-scale U.S. assistance to the develop-

4. See Keohane (1984, p. 142).
5. Rogowski (1989, p. 120).
6. Bergsten (1992, p. 3).

ing world was even more clearly a cold-war artifact. Walt W. Rostow, later a senior White House and State Department official, at one point spelled out the rationale for U.S. development aid to poor countries in an influential essay subtitled "A Non-Communist Manifesto."[7]

The unusual postwar circumstances also helped make outward-first leadership possible by temporarily weakening the relative power of Congress. Assertive congressional partisanship on foreign policy, of the kind that had earlier destroyed Wilson, gave way momentarily to congressional bipartisanship and deference. In the area of military security policy, the president (as commander in chief) was given unprecedented peacetime authority over the deployment and use of both conventional and nuclear weapons, and in the area of intelligence the president began to exercise essentially unsupervised authority over the secret actions abroad of the newly created Central Intelligence Agency.

The congressional posture of deference even reached into the arena of foreign trade policy, despite explicit language in the U.S. Constitution granting Congress the sole power to regulate commerce with foreign nations, and despite a long tradition in Congress of asserting district-level demands for industrial protection.[8] The president technically had been granted authority to negotiate and implement reciprocal tariff reductions abroad under the Reciprocal Trade Agreements Act of 1934, but it was not until World War II, when protectionist Republicans in Congress finally stopped blocking the president's liberal trade initiatives, that vigorous outward-first U.S. trade policy leadership became a domestic political possibility.[9]

Congressional deference to executive branch leadership in the area of foreign economic policy was then strengthened further during the early years of the cold war. The result was not a sacrifice of economic to security interests, because in practice there was little policy conflict between these two spheres; both interests could usually be pursued simultaneously, along separate institu-

---

7. See Rostow (1960).
8. The classic depiction of this tendency is provided by Schattschneider (1935).
9. See Destler (1992, p. 31).

tional tracks.[10] In some ways the cold war may have helped the country to pursue its foreign economic policy interests because it strengthened the power of the president to reject shortsighted domestic political demands from single sectors and from single industries.[11] The economic demands from Congress that tended to be weakened during the cold war reflected district-level rather than national-level economic interests. Congressional deference during the cold war gave greater operating freedom to economic policy technocrats inside the executive branch, who saw most clearly the link between generous outward-first leadership and long-term U.S. strategic and economic goals.

Just as important during this period, but just as circumstantial, was the unusual willingness of many other industrial nations to follow a U.S. lead. Some (such as West Germany and Japan) followed because they had recently been defeated and occupied by U.S. and allied armed forces, had experienced political reconstruction under U.S. and allied occupation and supervision, and felt themselves to be on the front lines of a new cold war against Soviet military intimidation. Germany's eastern sector and Japan's northern islands were occupied by potentially hostile Soviet forces, which left West Germany and Japan feeling heavily dependent on U.S. conventional and nuclear arms guarantees. Others (such as Britain and France) followed because they had been either defended or liberated in World War II by U.S. military arms, they too feared Soviet expansion, and they had imperial interests (from the eastern Mediterranean to Indochina) that they were no longer capable of defending alone.

Given such dependence of foreign governments on the United States, why was U.S. foreign economic policy so openhanded? So acute were cold-war concerns in the United States that it was judged safer to pay too much to ensure alliance solidarity than to risk a breach. The United States so deeply valued allied recovery

10. See Cooper (1972–73).

11. At an industry level, the national security issue can cut different ways. In export-oriented high-technology industries, security-motivated export controls may have cost U.S. companies $21 billion to $27 billion yearly. See Robert Keatley, "U.S. Rules Dating from the Cold War Block Billions of Dollars in Exports," *Wall Street Journal*, October 15, 1993, p. A7. Conversely, in the case of machine tools security arguments sometimes provide a justification for lucrative protection. See Prestowitz (1989, p. 407).

and diplomatic cooperation that it stopped insisting on the convertibility of the British pound, eased pressures on the Dutch, French, and British for dismantlement of colonial trade preferences, supported and promoted European integration, accepted discrimination against the dollar, brought Japan into the IMF and the General Agreement on Tariffs and Trade (GATT), and offered Japan highly favorable terms of access to the U.S. market.[12]

Passing of the Postwar Period

Most of the unusual circumstances that made generous outward-first leadership appropriate and affordable for the United States following World War II have now either been weakened, altered, or eliminated. The U.S. economy no longer has such relative strength, the executive branch no longer enjoys as much deference from Congress, and the security imperatives of the cold war have largely evaporated. Also, the very success of U.S. leadership in promoting a more deeply integrated postwar economy has now pushed the task of leadership into a new arena. Successful leadership in the area of international policy coordination must now include initiatives taken behind the border as well as at the border. The increasing need for internal policy initiatives undercuts some of the value of an outward-first leadership posture. I consider each of these changed circumstances in turn.

A Changed Economic Position

All of the western industrial powers together, including the United States, made fabulous absolute economic gains during the postwar era. In relative terms, however, the economic position of the United States measurably declined.

The first stage of this decline was actually intended, because it grew directly out of generous U.S. support for economic recovery in Europe and Japan. As these economies revived abroad, the margin of U.S. supremacy naturally narrowed. U.S. labor productivity fell from almost three times the world average in 1950 to just

12. Nye (1990, pp. 91–92).

one and one-half times the world average by 1977. Between 1950 and 1970 the U.S. share of combined U.S., European Community (EC), and Japanese output declined from 69 percent to 55 percent.[13] The U.S. share of international financial reserves fell from 49 percent in 1950 to just 7 percent by 1976.[14]

Optimists have argued that this relative U.S. economic decline stopped in the mid-1970s as the natural postwar recovery in Europe and Japan reached completion.[15] If the focus is primarily on U.S. shares of world production and trade, such optimism can to an extent be justified.[16] On the other hand, if U.S. trade and financial balances are selected as indicators, a significant relative decline continued at least through the decade of the 1980s.

During the decade of the 1980s, the United States transformed itself from the world's largest net creditor to the world's largest net debtor nation. In just three years following President Reagan's supply-side tax cuts in 1981, the entire net foreign asset position that three generations of Americans had accumulated since 1914 was dissipated, and in the three years after that the United States went on to accumulate the world's largest net foreign debt.[17] As a related effect, because consumption grew while public and private savings rates fell, the U.S. merchandise trade balance (which had been consistently positive from 1894 until 1970) also turned strongly negative in the 1980s, reaching annual deficit levels as high as $159.5 billion in 1987.[18]

13. GDP shares are calculated in Keohane (1984, p. 197).

14. See Krasner (1982, p. 38). The decline in financial reserves was somewhat less worrisome to the United States than some other countries because America was a key currency country.

15. See Nye (1990, p. 73).

16. Even by these indicators, however, optimism becomes harder to justify after the mid-1980s, when dollar exchange rates fell sharply. Calculating on the basis of current prices and exchange rates between 1985 and 1992, the U.S. share of all GDPs of the western industrial countries (the OECD countries) taken together fell from 45 percent to 32 percent. See OECD (1993, p. 172).

17. See Friedman (1989, p. 227).

18. Merchandise trade deficits alone were only a partial indicator because net returns on past U.S. overseas investments and a surplus in services offset a substantial part of that merchandise deficit. But the massive U.S. merchandise trade deficits that began to occur in the mid-1980s (described by former Federal Reserve chair Arthur F. Burns as "awesomely different" from anything that any country had ever experienced in the past) swamped even these offset effects and had to be financed with heavy borrowing from abroad. See Destler (1992, pp. 48–49, 60–61).

Financial and trade balances are imperfect indicators of the relative international economic strength of the United States, in part because they can change so fast, but the deterioration in these balances noted during the decade of the 1980s nonetheless undermined both the capacity and the incentive of the U.S. government to play a generous and outward-looking leadership role. Today U.S. officials have a relatively weaker hand to play abroad; they can put fewer assets on the bargaining table. Setbacks in the energy and technology sectors are also symptomatic. Since 1947 the United States has gone from being one of the world's largest exporters of petroleum to being the world's single largest importer. In technology and management skills, the United States still has much to give, but less in relative terms than it had during the early postwar period.[19]

As the relative economic position of the United States has weakened, incentives to lead abroad have also weakened because the relatively smaller U.S. economy now captures a relatively smaller share of any international public goods benefits preserved or created by the leadership process. A larger share of the benefit from those goods will now be captured by more rapidly growing economies abroad, especially in Asia and the developing world.

It may seem implausible, when looking at the high level of consumer affluence that prevails in the modern U.S. economy, to argue that the nation is no longer rich enough to bear the same leadership burdens abroad that it once bore. Consumer affluence, however, is part of the problem. Despite a weaker internal savings and investment position, the United States continues to spend more than any other country on personal consumption. In 1990 private consumption per capita in the United States was approximately 40 percent higher than in West Germany, the United Kingdom, or Japan.[20] It was to sustain such lavish personal consumption, especially in the 1980s, that the United States skimped

19. See Thurow (1992, p. 154).
20. OECD calculations, based on current purchasing power parities. See OECD (1992). In areas such as food consumption, housing, and ownership of automobiles, telephones, and television sets, the United States continues to outdistance the rest of the affluent industrial world. "Eight of ten U.S. teenagers have their own camera. Seven of every ten own a stereo." See Malabre (1987, p. 3).

on investments in future growth and weakened itself with large new internal as well as external debts. Consumer installment loans, which contributed only 2 percent to U.S. personal income in 1947, were making up nearly 20 percent of personal income by the mid-1980s. Mortgage borrowing by the mid-1980s had increased to roughly thirty times the 1950 level.[21]

Less Congressional Deference

A second changed circumstance is the passing of bipartisan congressional deference to the president in the area of foreign policy. Postwar deference began to weaken with the election to Congress, in the late 1950s and early 1960s, of a generation of younger and better educated senators and representatives. Members of this new generation eventually gained seniority, asserting themselves decisively against the executive branch in the mid-1970s when openings for congressional resurgence were provided by the Vietnam War and the Watergate scandal. As a part of its resurgence, Congress created two new internal support agencies, the Office of Technology Assessment and the Congressional Budget Office, roughly tripled personal support staff levels, and almost tripled committee staff. By the 1990s the House and the Senate together had more than 250 separate committees and subcommittees (giving virtually every senator and most representatives a senior position), which demanded roughly 5,000 separate reports from various executive branch agencies. The Senate required individual confirmation for more than 300 presidential appointees, more than double the number of 1960.[22]

Congressional resurgence did not immediately transform the substance of U.S. foreign economic policy because a strong majority in Congress still agreed with the prevailing executive branch preference for freer international trade.[23] As congressional seniority structures were altered, however, policy substance eventually

21. See Malabre (1987, pp. 3, 46, 27). Americans also hold more than 1 billion credit cards; the French hold only 19 million credit cards, the Germans only 5 million. See Spiro (1993, p. 187).
22. See Califano (1994, pp. 40–41); Huntington (1981, pp. 207–08).
23. See Pastor (1980, p. 341).

came to be threatened. Congressional reform efforts in the mid-1970s included a reduction in the power of senior members and committee chairs, who had played an important role until then in shielding less secure and more junior members from constituents' pressures to legislate industry-by-industry protection.[24] Congress thereafter became far more active in debating trade policy, and trade-restrictive legislation was more frequently introduced. Between the Ninety-sixth Congress (1979–80) and the One hundredth Congress (1987–88) the number of foreign trade measures referred to five key House committees increased by 60 percent, and multiple committee referrals proliferated.[25] Between 1975 and 1980 the frequency of House and Senate floor references to trade went up by 70 percent.

Trade liberalization was still the preference of most members of Congress, so new legislative procedures had to be improvised to ensure that trade-liberalizing initiatives could still be undertaken by the executive branch. Hence the development of today's fast-track procedure (originally a part of the 1974 Trade Act), which allowed the president to seek congressional implementation of negotiated nontariff trade agreements through a single deadline-driven vote, with no committee or floor amendments allowed. This new procedure was used to good advantage by President Carter and Trade Representative Robert Strauss in 1979, when it effectively restricted any after-the-fact congressional tampering with the negotiated results of the Tokyo Round of Multilateral Trade Negotiations in GATT.

As the U.S. trade deficit worsened in the 1980s, however, congressional assertiveness increased. In 1988, with twenty-three committees participating, Congress for the first time mandated trade actions against individually identified priority foreign countries under the so-called Super 301 provisions of the Trade and

24. As I. M. Destler has shown, powerful and secure trade committee chairs (such as House Ways and Means chair Wilbur D. Mills) had been a hidden key to preserving the postwar pattern of congressional deference on trade-liberalizing initiatives abroad. When the House Democratic caucus, in 1975, opened up the business of the Ways and Means Committee to more public scrutiny and participation by junior members, it inadvertently removed from ordinary House members their earlier freedom to tell demanding constituents there was nothing they could do about trade. See Destler (1992, pp. 28–30, 66–69).

25. See Nivola (1993, p. 98).

Competitiveness Act of 1988. This legislation, which was in effect during 1989 and 1990, set deadlines for remedial action by foreign countries whose trading practices were found "unfair"; the provisions were targeted primarily at Japan. The stated aim was to open foreign markets to U.S. exports, but through a threatened unilateral closure of U.S. markets.[26]

Fast-track authority also ceased providing as much leeway to the executive, as the periodic votes required to extend fast-track authority gave individual members who opposed liberal trade an additional chance to register their objections. Some members who were agnostic on trade issues also used those occasions to sell (or rent) their votes to the president for a price. In 1991, when President Bush had to seek extended fast-track authority to negotiate the North American Free Trade Agreement (NAFTA) with Mexico, he had to empty his pockets and tie his hands with promises in order to buy enough congressional votes for passage, and even then he was opposed by a majority of House Democrats. In 1993, when President Clinton submitted NAFTA implementing legislation to Congress under fast-track rules, he was barely able to prevail in the House even after buying dozens of votes with costly favors, often from one member or one district at a time. On this occasion it was necessary for Clinton to engineer after-the-fact changes in the text of the NAFTA agreement to buy House support, thereby undermining some of the international negotiating credibility that fast-track authority was intended to provide. By 1994 fast-track authority had become so unpopular in Congress that President Clinton felt obliged to postpone a request for its extension until after what he expected would be a close Senate vote on implementation of the Uruguay Round GATT agreement.

Lack of congressional deference on trade policy was even more visible in 1993 and 1994 when the Clinton administration found itself obliged, under new congressional budget rules, to find offsets for the tariff revenues that would be lost through trade liberalization agreements such as NAFTA and GATT. The 1994 congressional debate over GATT focused as much on the domestic budget effects of the accord as on the issue of open trade. In a

26. See Bergsten and Noland (1993, pp. 16, 229).

discouraging way, Congress was coming full circle on tariffs. Tariffs were again being treated, as they had been two hundred years earlier, more as inward-looking revenue instruments than outward-looking foreign economic policy instruments.

End of the Cold War

With the end of the cold war, the disappearance of a clear and compelling foreign security threat has also undermined the capacity of U.S. political leaders to muster domestic support for a variety of outward-first international actions.[27] President Bush, who was barely able to manufacture a domestic consensus before the 1990–91 Persian Gulf war, was surprised by how quickly his support evaporated after the United States prevailed in that war. By the end of 1991, as the traditional Soviet adversary finally dissolved, Bush found himself harshly criticized for not paying enough attention to domestic affairs. It was a symptom of the new era when Bill Clinton defeated Bush in the 1992 presidential election, despite his own weak credibility in the area of foreign policy and his virtual neglect of foreign policy issues during the campaign. Clinton's acceptance speech at the Democratic National Convention devoted only three paragraphs (out of eighty-five) to international issues.[28] Clinton's most important foreign policy promise in the campaign was a pledge to cut Pentagon spending by $60 billion more than President Bush had, hardly a sign that he intended to continue in an activist leadership posture abroad.

In his first year and a half as president, Clinton assigned clear priority to domestic issues. His first congressional address, in February 1993, was practically devoid of references to the world outside, and soon thereafter his under secretary of state, Peter Tarnoff, told diplomatic reporters that the new administration would "define the extent of its commitment" abroad in ways that

---

27. See Hastedt and Eksterowicz (1993).

28. One of the three paragraphs was an assertion that the end of the cold war should allow the United States to reduce defense spending and embrace a new doctrine—that "strength begins at home." Address reproduced in Clinton and Gore (1992, pp. 217–32).

"may soon fall short of what some Americans would like and others would hope for."[29] An insular mood in Congress reinforced this early executive branch inclination to withdraw. When eighteen U.S. soldiers were killed in Somalia in the fall of 1993, Congress forced Clinton to set a fixed date for the termination of U.S. involvement in the UN peacekeeping operations there, which created spillover pressures to limit U.S. actions in Bosnia and also for a time in Haiti. Clinton did block congressional rejection of the already completed NAFTA agreement in 1993, and in 1994 he pushed for implementation of the Uruaguay Round Agreement in GATT, but both predated his presidency; his inclination to launch new international initiatives was close to nil.

U.S. commercial diplomacy has remained active, but since the end of the cold war it has become markedly less generous, especially toward former cold war allies. With Japan, the post–cold war turnaround came late in 1991 when the Bush administration transformed what had originally been planned as a cooperative diplomatic summit meeting on Pacific security into a high-profile bilateral confrontation over sales of U.S. auto parts. When Clinton's secretary of state, Warren Christopher, traveled to Tokyo in April 1993, he used his first meeting with Japan's new foreign minister to ask if Japan planned to purchase more American personal computers. Early in 1994, U.S. officials threatened trade retaliation in language that implied Japan was now the enemy: "I think this is an ideal time to use psychological pressure," said a senior administration official. "If we put this relationship through a sufficiently protracted period of friction, I think they will sue for peace."[30]

In parallel fashion, the Clinton team opened its post–cold war relationship with former allies in Europe by threatening to impose $45 million in sanctions over a dispute about electrical and telecommunications procurement policy. U.S. Trade Representative Mickey Kantor explained this new approach: "The days when we could afford to subordinate our economic interests to foreign

29. See Thomas L. Friedman, "There's Nothing Like Foreign Policy for Producing Ennui," *New York Times,* June 13, 1993, p. E3.

30. Thomas L. Friedman, "Clinton's Japan Card?" *New York Times,* February 12, 1994, p. 4.

policy or defense concerns are long past."[31] This less cooperative attitude was institutionalized in Clinton's National Economic Council, which had been formed in part to ensure that economic disputes with former allies would be pursued aggressively rather than be subordinated to diplomatic concerns.[32]

U.S. economic policies in the developing world were also less generous after the end of the cold war. A National Security Council study of foreign aid policy options, prepared for President Clinton in mid-1993, stated flatly that "with the disappearance of communism in the Soviet Union and Eastern Europe, the bedrock support for foreign assistance has eroded significantly. There is no clear vision guiding the shape of our foreign assistance agenda for a world without the USSR."[33] Aid levels were thereafter cut sharply. Administrator J. Brian Atwood of the U.S. Agency for International Development (AID) explained that after the cold war the United States no longer needed an aid program to purchase influence abroad. In November 1993, AID announced that twenty-one of its foreign missions, serving thirty-five countries, would be closed in the next three years.

Clinton announced (over the objections of both AID and the State Department) that more of the remaining U.S. aid would be tied explicitly to the purchase of goods made in the United States. This represented abandonment of an earlier U.S. policy to block the use of foreign aid for pursuit of narrow mercantile trade objectives. Secretary of the Treasury Lloyd Bentsen, one of the supporters of this shift, explained it by saying, "I'm tired of a level playing field. We should tilt the playing field for U.S. business. We shoud have done it 20 years ago."[34] Generous outward-looking leadership thus gave way, in one setting after another, to a foreign policy focus that revolved mostly around short-term commercial self-promotion.

31. See "Cool Winds from the White House," *The Economist*, March 27, 1993, p. 58.

32. Council member W. Bowman Cutter, Clinton's deputy assistant for national economic policy, explained to the American Bar Association in April 1993 that the old paradigm that subordinated trade policy to military security issues had faded and that a new paradigm was being put into place. *Inside U.S. Trade*, May 17, 1993, p. 17.

33. Thomas W. Lippman, "Top US Panel Urges Reform of Foreign Aid, *Boston Globe*, September 18, 1993, p. 1.

34. Michael K. Frisby, "Clinton Weighs Linking Exports to Foreign Aid," *Wall Street Journal*, September 29, 1993, p. A2.

Diminished U.S. willingness to provide generous international leadership has been paralleled by diminished willingness on the part of former U.S. cold war allies to follow the United States. In Germany, because the Soviet menace was suddenly gone, because U.S. support was no longer needed to achieve reunification, and because cooperation within the European Union seemed more important, deference to U.S. preferences has declined. Germany repeatedly disappointed the United States in 1992 and 1993 by failing to push France toward honoring the original Blair House agreement on agriculture, struck between the United States and the European Union in 1992, which could have more quickly brought an end to the Uruguay Round of GATT negotiations. France itself, in a Europe no longer dominated by the two superpowers, has found greater room for exercising its penchant for independent action.[35] One of President Clinton's few original trade-liberalizing initiatives, an "Open Markets 2000" plan to follow up the 1993 Uruguay Round GATT agreement, was blocked by France at the July 1994 G-7 economic summit. Even the Japanese have become less deferential. Japan surprised the United States early in 1994 by allowing a summit meeting with President Clinton to fail rather than accept the Clinton administration's numerical indicators approach to correcting bilateral trade imbalances. Clinton responded by signing an executive order that revived the Super 301 provisions of the 1988 Trade Act, a clear threat of possible bilateral trade sanctions, yet Japan continued to resist numerical indicators. In May 1994 the United States had to agree to downgrade its insistence on numerical targets in order to restart the negotiations and in October 1994 had to accept an effective exemption of private sector trade from its numerical targets approach in order to reach a limited bilateral trade policy compromise with Japan (one which also excluded any gains in the auto and auto parts sector).

The post–cold war era is thus one in which a diminishing U.S. inclination to engage in generous outward-first leadership is matched by a diminishing inclination on the part of others to follow U.S.

35. See Hoffmann (1993).

leadership. Severe or escalating conflict need not be the result, but neither is this likely to be an era in which outward-first U.S. leadership can provide, as much as it did earlier, a foundation for continued international economic cooperation and still deeper economic integration.

A More Integrated World Economy

Today's more deeply integrated world economy also makes continuation of outward-first U.S. leadership difficult. Following World War II, reopening of the world economy required a mix of leadership actions taken mostly at the border (such as tariff reductions) or beyond the border (such as Marshall Plan assistance grants, technical aid to poor countries, or central bank interventions in international currency markets). In part because of the success of such initiatives, today's world economy has a somewhat different set of needs. Actions and adjustments at the border and beyond the border are still important, but as a result of the greater integration that has already been achieved, actions and adjustments behind the border will increasingly dominate the agenda of international economic policy.

For most of the post–World War II period the states of the industrial west managed to enjoy new wealth from expanding flows of cross-border trade and investment without having to give up too much of their traditional social policy autonomy. To some extent these states were willing to open their national economies at the border only because they thought they would continue to be permitted a full range of autonomous interventions behind the border.[36] Today the expansion of cross-border activity has reached a point that weakens the autonomous choice of policies behind the border. In order for the efficient expansion of economic activity to continue, policy adjustments will have to be made in traditionally domestic areas such as tax policy, environmental regulation, agricultural subsidies, social welfare policy, and labor relations.

36. See Ruggie (1982).

International leadership will remain essential to the management of behind-the-border policy adjustments, and most of that leadership must still come from the United States. Yet several distinctive features of the U.S. political system may make the exercise of this new policy leadership more difficult if attempted in an outward-first fashion, as discussed in chapter 4.

Chapter 4

Underlying Constraints on Outward-First U.S. Leadership

UNDERLYING features of the U.S. political system have always made outward-first leadership difficult. These distinctive institutional and cultural constraints were muted by the military security emergencies that existed during World War II and the cold war, but in the post–cold war era they may regain their traditional prominence.

Foreign observers have always appreciated the distinctive qualities of the U.S. political system better than the native born. The original skeptic regarding U.S. institutional preparedness for world leadership was the French aristocrat Alexis de Tocqueville, who in 1833 described American democracy as deficient in those characteristics necessary for success in foreign policy—patience, persistence in pursuit of a fixed long-term objective, and secrecy.[1] Such skepticism has remained alive to the present day, even among scholars who have witnessed the triumphs of U.S. postwar leadership.[2] Theodore Lowi concluded in 1979 that the problem for U.S. foreign policy had never been to make the world safe for democracy, but rather to make U.S. democracy "safe for the world":

---

1. See Tocqueville (1945, pp. 243–44).
2. For an extended examination of the assets and liabilities of U.S. foreign policy institutions, see Hoffmann (1968). Hoffmann concludes that the U.S. government is too complex and too sprawling to provide foreign policies that have the needed combination of unity and flexibility.

After thirty years of world leadership we must ask how a pluralistic democracy can adjust to the requirements of its world role. The interest-group-liberal, quasi-egalitarian requirement will never be conducive to modern foreign policy making. The autonomy of international agencies, the direct and intimate relationship of our plebiscitary president to his public, and the opportunities each has to influence the other, are as frightful for foreign policy as they would be attractive for domestic policy.[3]

Borrowing from Lowi and others, a list can be compiled of seven enduring and distinctive features of the U.S. political system that have always weakened the conduct of outward-first leadership: divided government; the powerful role of Congress, especially in trade policy; lack of unity and lack of continuity within the U.S. executive branch; the transparency and public penetration of executive branch policymaking; the dominance of courts, judges, and lawyers in U.S. foreign economic policy; the increasing power of state and local governments (federalism); and the persistently insular and inward-looking nature of U.S. political culture.

Divided Government

The two-hundred-year-old U.S. Constitution, which for all its virtues is still a preindustrial document, was never intended to ensure unified authority over the nation's economy. Even at the federal level the U.S. political system is different from an idealized Westminster parliamentary system, in which governmental unity and accountability are maintained by conferring all power upon the leadership of the majority party in parliament.[4] The U.S. federal government is constitutionally divided into three autonomous branches, and because the separately elected executive and legislative branches are so often divided by partisanship, it is often impossible to present a unified face to foreign governments. In

---

3. Lowi (1979, pp. 128, 162–63).
4. When the framers opted for a separation of powers they thought they were imitating a British constitutional characteristic, in contrast to the tyrannical French alternative. Outdated observations by Montesquieu, which still influenced the framers, contributed to this misperception.

twenty-six out of the forty-two years between 1952 and 1994 the presidency was controlled by the Republican Party while one or both houses of Congress were Democratic. The midterm election of 1994 left a Democratic presidency and a Republican Congress. The newly designated Republican chair of the Senate Foreign Relations Committee, Jesse Helms, appeared likely to oppose the president on issues ranging from UN peacekeeping and the biodiversity treaty to Uruguay Round implementation and foreign aid.[5]

The U.S. system, because of weak party discipline, tends to exacerbate conflict between the executive branch and Congress even when there is no partisan division. President Clinton nominally enjoyed a comfortable Democratic majority in the House of Representatives in 1993, but passage of his legislation to implement the North American Free Trade Agreement (NAFTA) was nonetheless a difficult struggle because both the House majority leader and the chief Democratic whip in the House actively opposed their own president.

Congressional Power over Trade

Even more constraining for outward-first leadership is a U.S. constitutional provision that grants all regulatory power over international commerce to Congress. This allocation of responsibilities made some sense in the eighteenth and nineteenth centuries, when the central purpose of U.S. tariff policy was inward-looking: to raise revenue for the government.[6] Today, when effective trade policy requires unified executive branch negotiation with governments abroad, it is hardly convenient that Congress still holds all formal authority.

To make this antiquated arrangement compatible with modern realities, it has been necessary for Congress to delegate power over trade policy to the executive through improvised devices such as

---

5. Divided government is not unique to the United States. France also elects its president and its legislature separately, and in the 1986–88 period its president and prime minister came from opposing ends of the political spectrum (a less extreme division returned following the election of 1993). See Milner (1993, p. 356).

6. As late as 1910 tariffs supplied about half of all federal revenues. See Destler (1992, p. 14).

fast-track authority.[7] Such improvisations have sometimes been able to restore a modicum of negotiating credibility to the executive branch, but not always. Executive branch officials signed a carefully negotiated "final" NAFTA text with Mexico in December 1992, but congressional reservations later obliged the Clinton administration—despite fast-track authority—to return to the Mexican government to demand another round of concessions. These included two supplemental agreements on labor and environmental protection, plus changes in the original agreement on trade issues such as sugar, citrus, wine, flat glass, and small appliances. At the time one European delegate to the General Agreement on Tariffs and Trade (GATT) drew a harsh conclusion: "What concerns me most is the price you have to pay to negotiate with the United States. In the first instance you've got to cut a deal, then you've got to cut a second deal to get it through the Congress."[8] Late in 1994, President Clinton's trade policy pronouncements prior to the Summit of the Americas were undercut because fast-track authority had, for the moment at least, expired.

Some argue that the dominant role of Congress in trade policy boosts U.S. credibility abroad because newly elected presidents are not able to change the policies of their predecessors without persuading Congress to agree to the change.[9] President Clinton, however, was not prevented from imposing after-the-fact changes in NAFTA on Mexico. Nor was President Reagan prevented, in 1981, from making abrupt changes in U.S. human rights, environmental, Law of the Seas, and tax policies.

Foreign governments can quickly become cynical. Shortly after his inauguration in 1993, President Clinton angered the European Union by criticizing and then appearing to reopen the terms of the bilateral U.S.–EU Aircraft Agreement (known as the Airbus deal) that had been concluded less than a year earlier

---

7. In the area of trade dispute settlement, delegation of congressional power has been more difficult to arrange. Congress has never considered itself bound by the international dispute settlement provisions of the General Agreement on Tariffs and Trade (GATT), an exclusion that weakens U.S. international trade policy leadership. See Porter and Vernon (1989, p. 14).

8. Quoted in Lawrence Ingrassia and Bhusha Bahree, "Nafta Victory Keeps GATT's Chances Alive," *Wall Street Journal*, November 19, 1993, p. A7.

9. Peter F. Cowhey has observed that "divided powers make it harder to initiate commitments and also harder to reverse them." See Cowhey (1993, p. 302).

by President Bush. Europeans pointed to this change and to the NAFTA change as evidence that the French were not being unreasonable in demanding to change the terms of the 1992 U.S.–EU Blair House agreement on reducing farm export subsidies. The Japanese were also wary about the credibility of U.S. presidential commitments. Following the signing, in July 1993, of an agreement on U.S.-Japanese trade by a-soon-to-depart Prime Minister Miyazawa, a Japanese finance ministry official who did not like the agreement is quoted as saying, "Maybe this time we can do what the Americans do, wait for a new administration, then disregard our past commitments."[10]

Congressional dominance in trade policy is also said to give more negotiating leverage to executive branch officials because they can point to the greater harm that Congress might do if maximum concessions are not made to U.S. negotiators. No doubt this stance at times provides a tactical advantage in extracting concessions, but it is not well adapted to undertaking clear and consistent executive branch initiatives, which are often the key to successful outward-first leadership.

Disunity and Discontinuity in the Executive

Disunity and discontinuity in the executive branch also constrain outward-first leadership options. The U.S. executive branch is less powerful than is the norm among executives in most other industrial countries, for idiosyncratic historical reasons. In the nineteenth century, at a time when centralizing state bureaucracies were expanding and growing stronger in Europe, the bureaucracy remained weak in the United States because of a prior spread of democratic political institutions (including locally based, patronage-oriented, congressionally centered political parties). The size and influence of the U.S. federal executive increased significantly during the first half of the twentieth century in response to two world wars and a deep economic depression, but far less than the parallel growth in the centralized administrations in Europe and Japan in response to the same events.[11] Consequently in the U.S. federal government there has been

10. David Wessel and Jacob M. Schlesinger, "Back-Room Deal: How the U.S., Japan Resolved Differences to Reach a Trade Pact," *Wall Street Journal*, July 12, 1993, p. A7.

11. See Ikenberry (1988, pp. 230–31).

no equivalent to the powerful central ministries of economic affairs, staffed by experienced career administrators, that are found in the bureaucracies of most other industrial states. The result has been less technical competence behind most U.S. foreign economic policies, less U.S. institutional memory, and less patience in pursuit of long-term U.S. objectives.

The U.S. federal government gives responsibility for the daily conduct of foreign economic policy to officials from a constantly changing stream of political appointees, roughly 3,000 in all, who come and go on a short-term basis, and whose average tenure in office is only two years. Hugh Heclo once labeled this revolving-door executive branch "a government of strangers."[12] Serious policy discontinuities are unavoidable; between 1981 and 1988 the U.S. Department of Commerce had four different assistant secretaries for trade and development.[13] Many political appointees come to office with no prior knowledge of one another, and frequently with inadequate technical knowledge. In 1993 President Clinton selected as his top coordinator for Uruguay Round (GATT) negotiations a former mergers-and-acquisitions lawyer who had important political ties to the mayor of Chicago but virtually no experience in trade policy; he selected as the leader of his bilateral Japanese trade negotiating team someone who had never been to Japan.

Because the larger professional ambitions of such appointees are often focused outside of government, these are not always effective team players. Rather than working quietly toward an interagency consensus, they often seek to make a quick mark for themselves through independent action, trying to end-run the laborious interagency consultation process by leaking privileged information to the press or by using personal ties to the president or to members of Congress.[14] Political appointees (and in some cases political consultants who do not hold official appointments) are thus constantly in competition with each other, battling for favorable press reviews or for the president's ear.[15]

12. Heclo (1977).

13. Prestowitz (1989, p. 429).

14. Prestowitz describes the resulting lack of teamwork: "I have often seen officials of one department fail to brief those of another department, or leak stories to the press, or attempt to bar a talented official from another department from a delegation, all in an effort not to surpass [foreign] opponents but to gain supremacy in the U.S. policy-making process" (1989, p. 430).

15. See Vernon, Spar, and Tobin (1991, p. 16); Woodward (1994).

Such competition among changing streams of political appointees is not all bad because it does ensure high levels of public participation in government. To foreign observers, however, this competition is often a source of confusion. Foreign governments looking to the United States for leadership cannot be sure how to interpret the pronouncements of executive branch officials. Words designed to win a continuing interagency argument may be mistaken for an already settled statement of government policy.[16]

Some have tried to portray this peculiar U.S. institutional attribute as a tactical advantage in dealing with nations abroad. Early in 1993, when conflicting official pronouncements on the new direction of U.S trade policy led to widespread confusion in Europe and Japan, Senator Max S. Baucus, chair of the finance committee's trade subcommittee, argued on the Senate floor that foreign confusion was good for the United States: "Do we really want to be predictable as we sit down to negotiate with our trading partners? Do we want them to know exactly what we'll do—and when? Or do we want to keep them guessing and get the best deal for our exporters?"[17] Foreign confusion may at times be an asset for getting the best deal in an adversarial negotiation, but it is seldom the best foundation on which to build outward-first international leadership.[18]

Efforts have repeatedly been made to correct for fragmentation and discontinuity in the executive branch through the creation of something like a national security council for international economics, but so far no cabinet-level interdepartmental council on foreign economic policy has survived a transition between administrations.[19] Eisenhower created the Council on Foreign Economic Policy (CFEP), which never met with the president, and which Kennedy abolished in 1961; Nixon created the Council on International Economic Policy (CIEP), which rivaled neither his National Security Council nor his Domestic Council, and which Ford

16. See Cohen (1982, p. 160).

17. "Clinton Tough on Trade But Policy Stays Blurred," New York Times, March 30, 1993, p. D2.

18. Fragmentation in the U.S. executive branch can also be a serious weakness in competitive negotiations with foreign governments if foreign governments are able to pick the U.S. agency they choose to deal with on the basis of which agency holds the most sympathetic view. See Prestowitz (1989, p. 426).

19. See Porter (1982, p. 182).

supplanted with the joint foreign-domestic Economic Policy Board (EPB); Carter abolished both the CIEP and EPB and created his own Economic Policy Group (EPG), which also failed to provide central control. Reagan abolished the EPG and created in its place the Senior Interagency Group on International Economic Policy, chaired by the secretary of the treasury; this council also proved ineffective and in 1985 was quietly disbanded.[20]

President Clinton's interagency National Economic Council (NEC) is yet another attempt to institutionalize better foreign and domestic economic policy coordination within the executive branch. In the post–cold war era Clinton's NEC has an advantage in not having to defer as quickly to international security and diplomatic policy institutions such as the National Security Council or the State Department. Yet the recent absence of a unifying foreign policy goal has made NEC coordination of the efforts of domestic and international cabinet agencies more difficult. For this reason, and because Clinton permitted every cabinet officer who asked to join the NEC to do so, the council had trouble, early in 1993, proposing a single framework to guide future U.S. trade negotiations with Japan. The council's original framework for negotiating with Japan contained five separate "baskets," or negotiating tracks, corresponding roughly to the five separate executive agencies (the Treasury, State, Defense, and Commerce departments and the U.S. Trade Representative's office) that had insisted on being involved.

Later in 1993, the National Economic Council was of some value in committing the Clinton executive branch to complete the already negotiated North American Free Trade Agreement. But the NEC then failed to impose unity on post-NAFTA trade policy in the hemisphere, so planning for the Summit of the Americas in late 1994 became badly fragmented. Throughout much of 1994 Latin American governments were not sure whether to follow the progress of an interagency review by the U.S. Trade Representative's office, or respond to a separate Treasury Department–State Department joint options paper, or place credence in Commerce Department initiatives presented to them in a series of public speeches.

Fragmentation of the U.S. political system can be significantly reduced in times of international crisis or confrontation. So occa-

20. Porter and Vernon (1989, p. 21).

sionally presidents are tempted to create an artificial mood of crisis in order to move policy forward. President Clinton resorted to apocalyptic warnings about the international consequences of failing to approve NAFTA to get the agreement through the House of Representatives in 1993, and he returned to this tactic again prior to the Uruguay Round vote in 1994. This tactic unfortunately heightens political tensions abroad as well as at home and runs serious risk of self-fulfillment.

Transparency of Policymaking

External policy initiatives are also constrained because U.S. procedures for making economic policy are uniquely transparent and subject to unusual public review and public participation. Detailed and timely information about policymaking in the United States is easy to obtain, thanks to the competitive dynamic in the executive branch and to the adversarial role of Congress. The "freedom of information" and legislative oversight obligations that are imposed by Congress on the U.S. executive branch vastly exceed those in systems with stronger permanent bureaucracies and without power separation. Interested private groups can follow executive branch decisionmaking in the United States almost on a day-to-day basis by subscribing to a relevant menu of private insider newsletters or carefully reading the specialized trade press.

The ready availability of information about executive branch policymaking (Congress exempts itself from most disclosure rules) allows deep penetration of the policy process not only by members of Congress and congressional staff but also by private sector lobbyists and citizens' groups. Since 1960 the number of interest-group representatives registered in Washington has increased from fewer than 500 to more than 6,000.[21] In Japan, where much less is publicly known about the daily workings of government, fewer citizens' groups have been able to organize effectively to penetrate and influence internal government processes.[22]

21. See O'Connor and Sabato (1994, p. 539).
22. For a comparative examination of the role of U.S. and Japanese nongovernmental organizations in environmental policy, see Pharr and Badaracco (1986, p. 258).

The transparency of and public participation in policymaking can help to ensure the legitimacy of and compliance with policies at home, but the cost is usually inability to conduct well-controlled and discreet interactions with governments abroad. Foreign governments that wish to deal effectively with the United States are frequently obliged to hire lobbyists of their own. Often such lobbyists are former or future U.S. officials, a further complication to the clarity and accountability of the process.

Some have argued that governments whose policymaking is transparent are more qualified than other governments to provide international leadership, because credibility can be boosted by the absence of mystery surrounding internal policy processes.[23] In the case of the United States, if a prior interagency consensus to support external policy is assumed, enhanced external credibility could be the result. When interagency consensus is lacking, however, transparency can make an outward-first approach chaotic.

Legalism in Policymaking

Although foreign economic policymaking in most other industrial countries is dominated by politicians, former business leaders, or technocrats (including professional economists), U.S. foreign economic policymaking often is dominated by courts, judges, and lawyers. This is particularly true of trade policy and external environmental policy.

Many final U.S. trade policy actions are decided upon neither by the Congress nor by the president, but instead by quasi-judicial institutions operating to some extent apart from both branches. U.S. trade law specifies that firms or workers who feel they are being injured by import competition or victimized by foreign trade practices can seek remedies (such as trade adjustment assistance or countervailing duties) from the U.S. International Trade Commission (ITC).

Such domestic trade laws have come to play a larger role since the decade of the 1970s, when U.S. interests facing competition

23. Cowhey (1993, p. 302).

from imports lobbied Congress successfully to broaden their eligibility to petition for remedies and tighten enforcements. Thereafter more petitioners sought relief under these statutes, and relief was more often obtained.[24] Between 1980 and 1987 the percentage of U.S. imports under special protection nearly doubled, from 12 to 23 percent.[25]

It has been noted that U.S. quasi-judicial procedures and remedies do not always undercut liberal trade policy, because they can sometimes mollify industry-specific grievances that would otherwise produce legislative demands for across-the-board protection.[26] In the eyes of foreign governments, however, the confusion and lack of accountability associated with these legal procedures is considerable. During the decade of the 1980s, at a time when the external commercial policies of Presidents Reagan and Bush were consistently geared toward open borders and trade expansion, the administration of U.S. trade law was frequently leading, on a case-by-case basis, to new import protections. Recent U.S. steel trade policy is a case in point. At the Group of Seven summit in Tokyo in July 1993, U.S. negotiators endorsed a Uruguay Round market access package that called for total elimination of steel tariffs, pending the conclusion of a multilateral steel agreement, but foreign governments were not impressed because only two weeks earlier the U.S. Commerce Department had independently announced provisional antidumping and countervailing duties on steel imports from twenty nations, sufficient to close the U.S. market to a wide range of foreign competition.[27] When European Community and GATT officials complained that the new U.S. duties on steel were a serious danger to the Uruguay Round, the Commerce Department argued that U.S. trade statutes allowed no

24. Destler (1992, p. 154).
25. Nye (1990, p. 206).
26. See Nivola (1993), especially chapter 4.
27. Poland was among the countries targeted, even though less than one-half of 1 percent of U.S. steel consumption was of Polish origin, and in spite of larger U.S. policy efforts to help the Polish economy. Vice President Albert Gore had visited Poland several months earlier and had praised the "green shoots of free enterprise springing up" in the country. See James Bovard, "Steel Rulings Dump on America," *Wall Street Journal,* June 23, 1993, p. A14.

room for "political" considerations and should thus be considered entirely separate from U.S. policy on the Uruguay Round.[28]

In the end, the independent operation of U.S. trade laws significantly weakened the outcome of the Uruguay Round on both sides of the Atlantic. Late in 1993 pressures by congressional friends of the steel industry and the semiconductor industry forced the administration to ask, at the last minute, for changes in eleven separate antidumping provisions in the 1991 Uruguay Round draft text. The purpose was to weaken international trade rules enough to ensure compatibility with the free exercise of U.S. domestic trade laws. One unintended result was a French demand for the creation of parallel antidumping laws in the European Union—laws strong enough to counter U.S. national laws.

Quasi-judicial trade law remedies in the United States have grown partly in response to a proliferation of nontariff industrial policy actions (such as subsidies or tax incentives) taken by other governments, especially in Europe. The United States has felt obliged to respond to such distortions, yet it cannot easily respond in kind because of a long-standing ideological aversion in the United States to explicit national industrial policies.[29] It has therefore responded by embracing haphazard quasi-judicial intrusions into the private sector, which have together proved almost as distorting, as well as frustrating to trade policy coordination.

The large role of law is also visible in U.S. international environmental policy. Domestic lawsuits are often the driving force behind U.S. external environmental relations. In U.S. relations with Mexico, the Bush administration was forced by a private domestic lawsuit (brought by the Earth Island Institute in 1990) to apply an import ban on Mexican tuna caught with purse seines, as required by the U.S. Marine Mammal Protection Act (MMPA), even though

---

28. This law-driven threat of a steel trade war was averted one month later when the ITC removed most of the tariffs that the Commerce Department had recently imposed. The ITC had found, under its own independent quasi-judicial procedures, that the imports had not been causing "material injury" to domestic industry. The independent ITC commissioners, however, were no more focused on the Uruguay Round than was the Commerce Department, explaining their actions as related to U.S. trade law rather than to U.S. trade policy. See Asra Q. Nomani and Dana Milbank, "Trade Panel Backs Foreign Steel Concerns," *Wall Street Journal*, July 28, 1993, p. A3.

29. See Martin (1993, p. 28).

a GATT panel would later find that the U.S. law violated international trade rules by allowing discrimination on the basis of production processes.

U.S.-Mexican relations were briefly upset again in 1993 when a federal district court ruled (in response to a lawsuit brought by Public Citizen, Friends of the Earth, and the Sierra Club) that President Clinton had an obligation to prepare an environmental impact statement for the NAFTA agreement. The Justice Department appealed the ruling, complaining that the court had intruded "on the president's inherent authority to conduct foreign affairs and enter into international agreements."[30] Later a federal appeals court reversed the decision; lawyers for Public Citizen planned to take the matter to the U.S. Supreme Court, and in February 1994 five environmental groups filed suit against the U.S. Trade Representative, in a different court, demanding that the Clinton administration complete an environmental impact statement on the GATT Uruguay Round agreement.

These GATT and NAFTA cases show that the power and reach of U.S. domestic legal processes can reinforce a tendency to uncontrolled public participation in the policymaking process. To challenge U.S. government policy, a private industrial association or a grass roots citizen's lobby need only file a lawsuit. There are more than 700,000 lawyers in the United States (compared with about 15,000 in Japan) eager to make the process of litigation widely available. Nearly three-quarters of all Washington-based lobbying groups engage directly in such litigation.[31]

Widespread and frequent litigation may boost public participation in policymaking, but it may also block the formation of a stable political or social consensus to support public policy. In the adversarial setting of the courtroom, contending parties are inclined to make extreme claims against one another rather than seek common ground, and the final judgment of the court, by offering victory to one party or another, is often temporary, pending appeal. Foreign governments wishing to anticipate the future direction of U.S. policy stand to be frustrated by such procedures;

---

30. "Clinton Pushes Drive to Wrap Up Side Deals on Free Trade Accord," *Wall Street Journal*, July 21, 1993, p. A6.

31. O'Connor and Sabato (1994, p. 551).

their only recourse may be to go into the U.S. court system with lawyers of their own.

An idiosyncratic tendency to legalism is also seen in the background and training of those officials who make foreign economic policy in the United States, among whom lawyers outnumber business executives, scientists, engineers, and economists. The original top foreign economic policy team of the Clinton administration featured eight agencies headed by lawyers (State, Treasury, Commerce, Labor, Agriculture, National Economic Council, Office of Management and Budget, USTR), and only one, the Council of Economic Advisers, headed by an economist. The president and the First Lady were lawyers as well, as were 45 percent of the members of Congress.[32] Through shared use of U.S. legal idioms officials may find it easier to communicate with each other, especially in guiding domestic policy processes, but the exclusiveness of U.S. law can be another barrier to effective interaction with foreign governments.

Federalism

An outward-first approach to economic policy leadership could also be frustrated in years ahead by the large and still growing role of state and local governments in the United States. The United States gives a prominent role to subnational governmental authorities, even when compared with other federal systems. As of 1989, state and local governments in the United States were responsible for 55 percent of social policy expenditures nationwide; in Germany, the European country often used to illustrate decentralized federalism, subnational governments were responsible for only 33 percent of all social expenditures.[33]

Once considered a shrinking realm of public authority, state and local government in the United States has been revived, relative to the federal government. This important revival dates from a series of state-level political reforms in the 1960s, led by court-mandated reapportionment of legislative districts. It gained new strength in

32. O'Connor and Sabato (1994, p. 183).
33. See United Nations Development Programme (1993, p. 71).

the 1980s, partly as a result of President Reagan's efforts to scale down the social actions of the federal government, which led to increased demands for expanded activity at the state and local levels. In one area after another—health, welfare, and the environment—the policy initiative shifted from the federal government to the states in the 1980s. Federal budget deficits, another legacy of the Reagan era, suggest that the shift in the locus of public authority away from the center will continue. Budget constraints helped defeat federal health care reforms in 1994; state governments with fewer budget constraints are now more likely to go forward with piecemeal subnational reforms. State and local governments are now generally in better financial condition than is the federal government, because of the tighter laws under which they have recently expended revenues and because of the successful efforts they have made to strengthen and diversify their revenue bases. Despite frequent taxpayer protests, state and local revenues (exclusive of federal grants) went up from 7.6 percent of GNP in 1960 to 10.3 percent in 1990; during the same period federal revenues (exclusive of social security taxes) fell as a share of GNP from 15.4 percent to 12.0 percent.[34]

Other realities also suggest that state and local governmental authority will continue to expand. Some of the most visible public needs in U.S. society today—including education, skills training, neighborhood security against crime, infrastructure repair, and child care—are better suited to management by state and local authorities than by a distant and financially paralyzed federal government. In this sense the future performance of state and local governments may determine whether or not U.S. society can compete successfully in the global economy of the twenty-first century. States are already taking a lead in devising policies to develop human capital, promote business-university partnerships, initiate site-specific infrastructure improvements, establish venture capital funds, and promote regional economies and exports.[35] The federal government is now poorly equipped both financially and institutionally to take on such tasks.

34. See Rivlin (1992, p. 107).
35. Rivlin (1992, pp. 120–21).

The growing strength and importance of state and local government in the United States is a healthy development. Yet it represents another constraint on outward-first leadership. As behind-the-border policy questions become more important, the federal government will find it increasingly difficult to initiate successful negotiations with governments abroad because it will be unable to speak for many state and local governments at home.

International government-to-government relations can sometimes be paralyzed by independent state actions in the United States. Consider the policy of the state of California (dating from the 1970s) to tax multinational firms on the basis of worldwide rather than local profits. This is arguably a policy with merit, yet it cuts across a thick web of international tax rule agreements and triggered lawsuits from foreign- and U.S.-based corporations and threats of retaliation from twenty foreign governments. Neither the president nor Congress found it easy to manage this dispute because the issue was under the jurisdiction of the California legislature and the U.S. Supreme Court (which in June 1994 upheld the tax by a 7 to 2 vote).

Even national trade policy can be constrained by state and local government. In completing the 1993 Uruguay Round of GATT negotiations, the federal government sought to gain greater access to telecommunications procurement in the European Union by offering to open up state-level procurement in the United States. When the federal government originally made this offer to the EU, it promised that all fifty states and all municipalities with populations of 500,000 or more would sign on; but as of April 1994 it had recruited only thirty-nine states, and only seven cities, that were willing to give up some or all of their "buy American" preferences. The National Conference of State Legislators demanded that the Clinton administration include in the Uruguay Round implementation bill a provision that would make federal and international challenges to existing state taxes or regulations more difficult under GATT. The 1993 NAFTA side agreement on environmental protection likewise had to be carefully drafted by the Clinton administration so as to disallow private legal challenges to existing U.S. state and local environmental laws.

If the relative power of state and local government continues to grow, federal officials may develop sympathy for the beleaguered officials of the European Union, who must fight against the inclination of the governments of member countries to conduct independent economic policies at home and abroad. Already it is common in the United States to speak of the governments of individual states and even municipalities as conducting their own foreign policies.[36] None of this need be harmful to the quality of government in the United States, but it will make outward-first U.S. leadership in economic policy more difficult.

An Insular Popular Culture

Despite two generations of experience with international leadership, many Americans remain ill-informed about the world outside. Gaps in their knowledge are too often filled with a self-satisfied belief that the rest of the world, if given a chance, would want to be more like the United States.

Such attitudes of insular self-satisfaction did not prevent the United States from being an effective outward-first international leader during the early postwar period, when many followers did in fact wish to be more like the United States—and depended heavily on the United States for assistance and protection. But these attitudes could be harder for followers abroad to accept in the post–cold war era of more equitable multilateral diplomacy.

The self-satisfaction and insularity of U.S. popular culture is reflected in how little most Americans think or know about foreign countries. A survey of television offerings in 100 nations, undertaken by the United Nations Educational, Scientific, and Cultural Organization (UNESCO), showed the United States last in the amount of time devoted to international items.[37] When asked to

36. According to one count in 1991, 27 different states and 126 separate municipalities had divested more than $20 billion from firms doing business with South Africa. International sister-city relationships had also proliferated, and at least ten large cities had their own funded offices of international affairs—in effect, their own state departments. See Shuman (1992).

37. See Simon (1980, p. 10).

name the two most important issues facing the United States, only 3 percent of the respondents to a *Los Angeles Times* poll in December 1993 mentioned any foreign issues at all.[38] American ignorance of foreign geography is legendary: a recent *National Geographic* survey revealed that 45 percent of Americans did not know where Central America was, and that less than 50 percent could find the United Kingdom, France, South Africa, Vietnam, or Japan on a map. Americans between the ages of 18 and 24 scored worse than their counterparts in each of the eight other countries surveyed.[39]

Ignorance about the outside world is compounded by the low standard of foreign language training in the United States. Over the past century, even as U.S. involvement in the outside world has deepened, foreign language training in the United States has deteriorated. In 1915, 36 percent of U.S. high school students were studying a foreign language, whereas by 1976 only 18 percent were doing so. In 1915, 85 percent of the nation's colleges required students to pass a competency test in a foreign language before admission, but by 1975 only 10 percent of the nation's colleges and universities even required records showing that a foreign language had been taken. Over the brief period between 1963 and 1974, the number of students enrolled in college foreign language programs declined by 44 percent. Of those who now graduate from public high school in the United States, fewer than 4 percent have had more than two years of foreign languages, whereas in France all students take at least four years of a foreign language.[40]

Weakness in language skills is visible at the highest levels of the U.S. government. Clyde V. Prestowitz, former counselor for Japan affairs to the U.S. secretary of commerce, has asserted that only about 10 percent of the U.S. embassy staff in Tokyo in recent years has been able to speak any Japanese, and only one or two individuals have been truly fluent.[41] In the years ahead language-poor U.S. officials may not be able to perform the difficult information-gathering and communications tasks necessary for outward-first leadership, particularly in regard to behind-the-border policy coordination.

38. *Los Angeles Times,* December 10, 1993, p. A22.
39. See Dertouzos and others (1989, p. 84).
40. Simon (1980, pp. 1–3).
41. Prestowitz (1989, p. 436).

The insularity of U.S. culture is explainable by both history and geography. The large size of the United States, combined with its distance from rival power centers across two oceans, has tended to make the United States a world apart.[42] The shedding of visible ties to foreign lands, languages, and cultures in order to become "American" long served immigrants as the best way to make themselves acceptable to established U.S. elites.[43] The insularity of U.S. culture was further strengthened by U.S. military and economic preponderance following World War II. So large and dominant was the U.S. economy at mid-century, and so attracted were foreigners to anything American, that Americans themselves momentarily felt less need to learn from, or learn about, the world outside. The learning burden (and hence the long-term learning advantage) was thus shifted to foreigners.

As a result, a serious problem of parochialism developed, particularly in U.S. business firms. U.S. corporate leaders, reading only English-language scientific, technical, and marketing journals, progressively lost touch with the growing strength of their foreign competitors and with the changing tastes of their foreign customers.[44] Today the Securities and Exchange Commission (SEC) enforces U.S. business accounting standards (erroneously called the Generally Accepted Accounting Principles) that were written in an era when U.S. securities markets could operate in isolation from the rest of the world. As a result, the trading of some world-class company stocks may now be driven into foreign markets.

Efforts have been made to reduce the insularity and parochialism of U.S. culture, but a turnaround remains elusive. Twenty-five years have passed since Congress decided that the United States should move toward use of the metric system. Despite the Metric Study Act of 1968, the so-called Metric Conversion Act of 1975, and an act signed by President Reagan in 1988 that specified the metric system as the preferred system of measurement for trade

42. By way of contrast, the much smaller states of Western Europe have remained highly sensitive and adaptive to their external environment. See Katzenstein (1985).

43. Americans tend to identity themselves in terms of distinctive national institutions and political values rather than in racial, social, geographical, or cultural terms. See Huntington (1981, p. 25).

44. Dertouzos and others (1989, p. 50).

and commerce in the United States, most daily measurements continue to be made in gallons, pounds, and miles. The only other countries in the world holding out so strongly against the metric system are Burma and Liberia.

At an elite level, U.S. culture is undergoing considerable internationalization. Private companies, foundations, leaders in state and local governments, and private individuals (as both professionals and tourists) are more deeply involved in the world outside than ever before. Some mild internationalization has also taken place just below the elite level, as travel abroad for the middle class has become easier and as more Americans have gained the broadening experience of a college education. These welcome social developments have so far found their most effective expression through private or local and regional channels, however, rather than through national policies.[45]

Insularity and self-absorption are now being worsened by domestic budget politics. In U.S. trade policy one source of trouble is a pay-as-you-go rule that came out of the U.S. domestic budget accord in 1990, requiring all new policies that lose revenue to be offset by a corresponding spending cut or tax increase. This domestic budget rule is now a major impediment to U.S. trade policy because it requires that any new tariff reductions at the border be met with corresponding budgetary offsets. In 1993 an important and long-standing U.S. trade preference commitment to the nations of the developing world, the Generalized System of Preferences, was momentarily terminated under this inward-looking rule because of $790 million in forgone tariff revenues. Later the Clinton administration found itself legally obliged to raise taxes to compensate for the loss of $2.3 billion in tariff revenues (over five years) that might result from NAFTA—which made it more difficult to secure congressional support for NAFTA.[46]

A more serious problem emerged in 1994 when Clinton was obliged to find funds to offset an estimated $11.5 billion in tariff revenues that would be lost during the first five years of the Uruguay Round GATT agreement. To reduce this offset obliga-

45. Michael Clough endorses this more privatized, decentralized, and regionalized approach to international leadership. See Clough (1994).

46. Lanier (1993); Lawrence (1993).

tion from ten years to five, Clinton was also obliged to seek a waiver from Senate rules, which increased to sixty the Senate votes needed to implement the agreement. It mattered little that the Uruguay Round agreement was almost certain to increase total federal tax revenues through stimulation of economic growth. The Clinton administration felt constrained from seeking a further waiver from the five-year budget requirement, given fears that had been expressed of the likely reaction in financial markets to any slackening of budget discipline. Domestic labor and environmental groups opposed to the Uruguay Round implementing legislation gained tactical strength from these domestic budgetary rules.

Conclusion

In sum, the U.S. political system is marked by important cultural and institutional barriers to the successful conduct of outward-first economic policy leadership. U.S. policymakers were able to overcome these barriers during much of the cold war era, because of an unusual combination of circumstances, particularly the sense of an external security threat. In the post–cold war era, without such factors at work, these barriers are more constraining.

I do not argue that the U.S. political system is unique, among industrial countries, in presenting such barriers to successful outward-first leadership. Behind-the-border institutions in Japan are certainly as distinctive, and Japan's cultural outlook in its own way may be as insular as that of the United States. The European Union (EU), as a collectivity, finds it even harder than the United States to maintain internal unity and to make and keep international commitments. Germany, the leading state within the EU, probably exceeds the United States in its embrace of internal political institutions that diffuse power. Canada gives more wide-ranging internal regulatory powers to subnational institutional authorities than does the United States.

These comparisons indicate that outward-looking followership may be almost as difficult to arrange in the years ahead as outward-looking leadership. It seems that the governments of all modern industrial democracies are better suited to the maintenance of accountability at home than abroad. The political institutions that govern today's advanced democracies may be increasingly well suited to a diffuse leadership style, an inward-first style based on initiatives that begin inside separate political systems and then move from system to system through subsequent international negotiations or through informal mechanisms such as imitation or response to market pressures.

Chapter 5

U.S. Suitability for
Inward-First Leadership

*I*N SEVERAL RESPECTS U.S. political and social circumstances make
the country well suited to inward-first leadership: the United
States is large, so its domestic policy actions can have large and
positive effects on the world economy and the global environment;
it is highly visible, so its domestic successes (and failures) are
noticeable abroad.

Although the U.S. economy is no longer sufficiently dominant
to sustain the many generous outward-first policy initiatives that it
once did, it is large enough to have a strong positive influence
abroad when operated properly at home. Because the United
States is still home to roughly one-third of all economic activity in
the western industrial world, the sound internal management of
the U.S. economy should be seen as uniquely valuable to the world
economy at large. David E. Spiro has written that "the United
States still has the largest economy in the world, and so what is
good for the United States is still by and large good for the stability
of the international political economy. If the United States can
clean its own house, then international finance and international
monetary stability will benefit."[1]

U.S. leaders who look inward will not be ignoring the world
outside because the U.S. economy is now so deeply integrated into
the world economy. Internal economic signals in the United States,
such as commodity price trends and interest rate movements, are

1. Spiro (1993, pp. 185–86).

54

to a greater extent than before a reflection of what is happening internationally. Between 1950 and 1990 the exported share of U.S. goods production increased almost threefold, from 6.3 percent to 18.2 percent;[2] between 1970 and 1987 foreign investments in U.S. stocks, bonds, and other assets increased from $107 billion to $1.5 trillion; and in 1985–87 the United States financed 60 percent of its net national investment from abroad.[3] Such developments have made it impossible for U.S. policymakers to ignore foreign interest rates and business cycles, even when looking inward.

The United States, with its relatively young, experimental, and multiracial culture, remains a highly visible political and social laboratory for the rest of the world. Its visibility is enhanced worldwide through films (of the world's 100 most-attended films in 1993, 88 were American) and television (the U.S.-based Cable News Network reaches two hundred countries, presenting a U.S. viewpoint in English and an abundance of news about the United States).[4] Thus when U.S. cultural innovations and domestic policy actions are successful, a powerful example is communicated to other societies. Innovations that may have originally been intended for internal use in the United States, such as environmental impact assessments and legislation guaranteeing equal employment rights for women, can quickly spread to other nations. It is notable that after environmental impact assessments were introduced by domestic legislation in 1969, the United States repeatedly tried to spread this innovation internationally through formal treaty, without success. Yet through informal imitation some thirty other countries had adopted such legislation by 1990.[5]

The unique opportunity for the United States to set (and implicitly harmonize) international standards by domestic example is to some extent being squandered today because of the growing visibility within U.S. society of racial conflict and marginalization, social and family breakdown, and urban violence. European and

2. Destler (1992, p. 45).
3. Nye (1990, pp. 217, 251).
4. See Auletta (1993, pp. 25–30). Currently, 40 percent of the 24-hour newscast on CNN International, from Monday to Friday, is recycled from CNN's domestic news.
5. The imitative transfer of innovative norms and policy institutions across cultures is well known to historians and social geographers. Arnold Toynbee described it as *mimesis*. See Sand (1990, p. 25).

Japanese officials now cite such problems in the United States as reasons not to follow the U.S. lead in social and economic policy.[6] Perhaps only by turning inward to address such failings at home can the United States retain an important influence on international standards. One advocate of this view has been Jeffrey E. Garten: "The time has again come to work on our own institutions before becoming enthusiastic exporters [of those institutions]. It's not that we should avoid promoting our values abroad forever. But how can we offer the American model to others when it is so tarnished at home?"[7]

Options in Fiscal, Agricultural, and Environmental Policy

The positive assets and attributes that make the United States well suited to inward-first leadership can be usefully examined in the context of the kind of behind-the-border economic policy issues that are likely to challenge U.S. leadership in the years ahead. Three such policy areas are reviewed here: fiscal policy coordination, agricultural policy reform, and environmental policy cooperation.

Looking only at behind-the-border issues risks misjudging how much has changed in the management of some traditional at-the-border issues (such as tariff and quota restrictions on trade) and some beyond-the-border issues (such as open-ocean fishing rights). For these issues (and others) an outward-first approach no doubt remains preferable. For the behind-the-border issues examined here, however, the outward-first ap-

6. In 1993 the foreign minister of Denmark rejected the U.S. example as a solution to Europe's jobs crisis: "I wouldn't advocate anything that resembles the U.S. model. In the U.S. we are seeing severe defects, social problems, crime and hopelessness in large urban areas. It's not something we should be encouraged to do. It's not the way to go." See Charles Goldsmith and Peter Gumbel, "EC, Its Competitiveness Waning, Argues Over Trimming Safety Net," *Wall Street Journal*, June 22, 1993, p. A10.

7. See Garten (1992, pp. 224–25). Garten's book was written before he joined the Clinton administration as a senior trade official.

proach has faltered and more promising inward-first options have arisen.

Fiscal Policy

How can the United States best lead the world in the conduct and coordination of national budget policies and in the harmonization of budget policies with other national macroeconomic policies? Fiscal policies are frequently seen as requiring some prior international coordination because they can have large effects across national borders in today's integrated world economy.[8] It is also commonly assumed that international coordination should take place in an explicitly outward-first fashion, with coordinating techniques ranging from institutionalized policy surveillance and regular consultations to formal or informal agreements among treasury ministers and central bank governors, all within a setting such as the Group of Seven (G-7) industrial countries. Enthusiasts for this approach frequently argue for further strengthening the international institutions that have grown up around the G-7 process. John Ikenberry has argued for creation of a G-7 secretariat and council of ministers, supported by intergovernmental and private sector consultative bodies, so as to widen and deepen the institutional infrastructure for macroeconomic policy coordination and agreement.[9]

Several justifications might support this outward-first approach. The first is a hope (or perhaps an economist's dream) that government technocrats would be able to agree on the one set of common fiscal and macroeconomic policies needed at any particular time to serve the common need. Such a technically correct policy set would then presumably sell itself to political leaders and domestic parliaments. However, even if political leaders worldwide wanted to

---

8. Dobson (1991) summarizes the most familiar justification for coordination: "The basic logic of economic policy coordination is that, in an increasingly integrated world, the policies of one government can spill over to affect the goals of others, and therefore governments should consult one another and attempt to coordinate their actions so as to take these linkages into account. They should then be better off than if they had acted independently" (p. 7).

9. See Ikenberry (1993, p. 136).

make policy choices on purely technocratic grounds, uncertainties regarding the technical accuracy of today's economic models could render international coordination difficult, risky, and possibly counterproductive.[10]

A better justification for outward-first coordination might be admittedly a political one: a preemptive international agreement on budget discipline, for example, could be used to isolate or weaken opponents of budget discipline at home. This justification is offered by Henry Owen, ambassador-at-large in charge of G-7 summitry during the Carter administration. As a means to balance the U.S. budget by the year 2000, Owen has proposed negotiating an international agreement, to be monitored by the International Monetary Fund, that would limit various national budget deficits to fixed percentages of GDP. Owen gives a familiar political argument for going abroad first: "Most of the G-7 heads of government want to limit their budget deficits but are having trouble doing so. They might welcome the leverage that such an international agreement could provide."[11] Some enthusiasts for this strategy have proposed that it be institutionalized through congressional commitments in advance to an up-or-down vote within ninety days on any fiscal policy commitments that U.S. presidents might make in the context of a G-7 summit.[12] The intent would be to create fast-track approval for international fiscal policy agreements somewhat akin to the fast-track procedure recently available for trade policy.

A third justification for an outward-first approach to fiscal discipline might be to correct the error made in 1981 when President Reagan embraced destabilizing supply-side tax cuts in an inward-first fashion. Perhaps such mistakes would not have been made if fiscal policy had been managed at the time with an outward-first approach.

Weak budget discipline within the United States did not begin with Reagan's 1981 tax cut; it had been a major problem at home and abroad since the mid-1970s. The U.S. debt-to-GDP ratio fell

10. See Frankel and Rockett (1988). For a more positive view of the model uncertainty problem, see Bryant (Forthcoming).

11. See Owen (1994, p. 171).

12. See Destler and Henning (1989, p. 163).

steadily for three decades after 1945 as wartime debts were slowly repaid, but it began rising in the mid 1970s and since then has more than doubled, from a low of 25.0 percent in 1974 to 59.6 percent by 1993. This loss of budget discipline could be traced partly to divided government in the 1980s. Congressional Democrats failed to curb spending (real spending on transfer payments climbed by approximately 30 percent during the decade), and Republican presidents refused to restore the revenues lost through the 1981 supply-side tax cut (a dozen revenue increases were subsequently enacted by Reagan and Bush, but less than two-thirds of the lost revenues were restored). With internal political accountability thus weakened by divided government, the annual U.S. fiscal deficit (excluding social security) increased from $74 billion in fiscal year 1981 to $238 billion in fiscal year 1986.[13] Because these large deficits were combined in the 1980s with a falling rate of private U.S. savings, they helped bring on high real interest rates at home and abroad, serious deterioration in the U.S. current account balance, and wide swings in currency exchange rates, all of which badly disrupted worldwide investment, growth, and trade.

These problems were primarily "made in the USA." They had been brought on by domestic policy actions, and they called for an inward-first remedy. Repeatedly during the latter half of the 1980s, however, the U.S. administration tried to manage these problems with an outward-first approach, going into international settings such as the G-7 to strike bargains on macroeconomic coordination with other governments. As a means to restore budget discipline in the United States these outward-first efforts were largely unsuccessful and may have weakened U.S. budget discipline further by making it easier for domestic political leaders to blame continuing economic imbalances on foreigners. In the G-7, outward-first efforts by the United States to persuade West Germany and Japan to reflate and to purchase more U.S. goods often served as a means to disguise the failings of U.S. domestic fiscal policy, thus postponing the politically painful correction of those failings.

13. See Schick (1993, pp. 201–06).

The best political opportunity to correct U.S. budget failings during the Reagan presidency came in 1985, following Reagan's landslide reelection, when the nation's economy was recovering strongly from recession. Reagan, a popular leader with no more elections in his future, might at that point have expended some domestic political capital to restore lost tax revenues and to secure a reduction in untargeted entitlement spending.[14] Instead, he opted for a less than courageous tax reform bill, which was designed from the start as revenue neutral.

It fell to the president's foreign economic policy team to compensate for this domestic fiscal lapse. Treasury Secretary James A. Baker III tried to make the best of the situation by launching an ambitious macroeconomic policy coordination initiative abroad. This was part of a larger pattern of outward-first international economic leadership during Reagan's second term on issues such as trade (the Uruguay Round) and debt (the Baker Plan). The trade and debt initiatives fared better than the macroeconomic coordination initiative.[15]

The macroeconomic policy coordination initiative began with the Plaza Agreement of September 1985, under which coordinated central bank interventions helped to sustain a fall in dollar exchange rates that was already under way.[16] At the Tokyo economic summit in May 1986, however, Baker went farther by pushing the G-7 to adopt joint surveillance of national macroeconomic policies, which was to include regular international meetings at the ministerial and deputies' levels as well as reports by treasury ministers to heads of government at future economic summits.[17] The stated purpose was to make governments more accountable to one another for their own domestic macroeconomic policies.

Economists with experience inside government worried immediately that the practical effect of internationalizing fiscal policy

14. See Nau (1990, p. 257).

15. Benjamin M. Friedman argued at the time that U.S. fiscal policy failings undermined the trade and debt initiatives: "America's refusal to correct its fiscal imbalance has been a major cause of the shallowness of these efforts at international policy coordination." See Friedman (1989, p. 16).

16. The Plaza Agreement was a formal agreement reached among G-5 finance ministers and central bank governors at the Plaza Hotel in New York City to attack exchange rate misalignments, partly by selling dollars for yen. See Destler and Henning (1989, p. 42).

17. Dobson (1991, pp. 41–42).

could be a further loss of budget discipline in the United States. Martin Feldstein, a former chair of the Council of Economic Advisers, argued that institutionalizing the surveillance of everyone else's policies abroad would give timid U.S. fiscal leaders another excuse for inaction at home.[18] The U.S. government might find another means to escape domestic political accountability by invoking concepts such as international burden sharing or complaining about alleged macroeconomic policy shortcomings in Japan and West Germany. This would also weaken accountability among the G-7 governments.

In retrospect, these misgivings were well founded. The United States employed the new international surveillance process to pressure Japan into fiscal expansion in 1986 and 1987 and to pressure West Germany into stimulating domestic demand in 1987 and 1988, but failed to deliver on its own promises to tighten fiscal policy at home.[19] Market effects then made matters worse, because the induced stimulation in Japan and West Germany gave the United States still more leeway in foreign exchange markets to keep its own undisciplined fiscal policies in place.

The tendency of international fiscal policy coordination (if led by an internally undisciplined state) to move systemwide in the direction of less discipline has been labeled by Vito Tanzi as the fox-without-a-tail syndrome: "As Aesop tells us, the fox that lost its tail tried to convince the other foxes that a tail was a burden after all, and the other foxes would be better off if they cut theirs off. International coordination of fiscal policy inevitably creates pressures on those countries that have been more successful in recent years in correcting their fiscal imbalances to relax their fiscal policy to bring it more in line with that of countries where less adjustment has taken place."[20]

18. See Feldstein (1988); Feldstein, ed. (1988); and Frankel (1988). For a brief challenge to this line of thinking, see Bryant (forthcoming).

19. Dobson (1991, p. 96). Randall Henning argues that the G-7 process had litle effect on West German and Japanese policy. See Henning (1994). Dobson's analysis of the coordination process details the extent to which Japan and West Germany met their commitments during the 1985–89 period and the United States failed to meet its own commitments.

20. See Tanzi (1989, p. 26).

Outward-first coordination, in part because it underperformed in regard to fiscal policy, placed excessive reliance on the use of monetary and exchange rate policies. Outward-looking policymakers in the executive branch find these policies easier to manipulate. Fiscal policy in the United States is dominated by Congress and is thus inherently difficult for the executive branch to coordinate abroad. Monetary and exchange rate policies, on the other hand, are somewhat insulated from congressional control and from partisan domestic politics. Monetary policy is formulated and conducted by the U.S. Federal Reserve, an agency independent by law, and exchange rate policy is typically controlled by a relatively small circle of senior technocrats in the U.S. Treasury Department. The ease of manipulating U.S. monetary and exchange rate policies can lead, within the outward-looking G-7 process, to excessive reliance on monetary stimulus or restraint and to excessive intervention by treasuries and central banks in foreign exchange markets. Former West German economic minister Count Otto Lambsdorff made this point in 1986: "The U.S. budget deficit is and will continue to be a destabilizing factor on the foreign exchange markets. To a large extent it shifts the burden of economic tuning onto monetary policy, which is too much for this one instrument to handle."[21]

Monetary policies may be well suited to tasks such as achieving and maintaining price stability, but they are not well suited to the correction of international imbalances because their effects on the current account can be offsetting. (Less domestic absorption will come from tight money, thus stemming imports, but a currency appreciation will also occur, which stems exports.)

Interventions in the foreign exchange market proved to be a poor substitute for fundamental macroeconomic policy change in the United States. Particularly in 1989, when intervention was used as a substitute for further action on the U.S. budget deficit, temporary success only contributed to complacency about U.S. fiscal policy.[22] As Destler and Henning have argued, "If currency market intervention and declarations are to have lasting effect, they

21. Cited in Nau (1990, p. 275).
22. See Dobson (1991, p. 140).

must be reinforced by macroeconomic actions, in the fiscal as well as the monetary area."[23] Because parallel fiscal actions were absent in the United States in the late 1980s, the outward-oriented macroeconomic policy coordination exercises of the period came to resemble a global effort by election-conscious political leaders to pressure central bankers into financing too much government debt.

Political leaders in the United States shed some of their complacency about the nation's budget deficit during the 1992 presidential election campaign when the federal deficit reached $290.2 billion, and two presidential candidates—first Paul Tsongas and then H. Ross Perot—enjoyed surprising success by adopting budget deficit reduction as their leading cause. The Democratic candidate, Bill Clinton, responded with a pledge to cut annual deficits in half within four years.[24]

Once elected, Clinton decided to make fiscal deficit reduction the centerpiece of his first-year domestic economic program. Because divided government had temporarily ended with the 1992 election, he knew he would be held more to account for fiscal policy discipline than any of his immediate predecessors were. Yet he sought to recover that discipline through an inward-first rather than an outward-first policy process.

Clinton's inward-first approach went against the advice of some traditionalists, who argued that explicit coordination with other governments still deserved priority. C. Fred Bergsten, founder of the Institute for International Economics, advised Clinton to convene an early G-7 economic summit conference at which U.S. policies could be designed as part of a larger multilateral package. Bergsten recommended such an outward-first approach because "all industrial countries are suffering from each other's weaknesses."[25] Henry Owen, as noted above, called for negotiation of a formal international fiscal policy agreement to be monitored by the IMF.

---

23. Destler and Henning (1989, p. 147).

24. Fiscal 1992 deficit of $290.2 billion from *Economic Report of the President, 1993*, p. 435, table B-74. Clinton and Gore (1992, p. 4).

25. Bergsten's proposal is reported in Terence Roth, "Dunkel Says a GATT Accord Is Unlikely Before March 'Fast Track' Deadline in U.S.," *Wall Street Journal*, February 1, 1993, p. 2.

Rejecting such proposals, Clinton went first to Congress with a proposal he characterized as good for the United States no matter what others did abroad. Only later, when he had provisional congressional endorsement of his domestic proposal in hand, did he go abroad to seek international cooperation through instruments such as the G-7.[26]

President Clinton's economic policy speech to Congress in February 1993 was inward-looking. It made occasional reference to international market forces but contained no references to the Group of Seven, other governments, or the economic policies of those governments. The president's centerpiece proposal to secure $500 billion in federal deficit reduction over five years was not described as contingent on foreign or international burden sharing. That proposal was soon criticized for its failure to switch enough federal spending from untargeted entitlement transfers to investments and for suggesting that significant new revenues could be gained by imposing higher taxes only on the rich. Clinton's goals nonetheless won popular favor, and by March 1993 a broad outline of the Clinton plan, including its $500 billion deficit-reduction target, had overcome partisan Republican opposition in a key vote in the House of Representatives. This budget action was so inward-looking that the economic policies of the other G-7 countries went virtually unmentioned in the debate.

Only after Clinton had preliminary congressional endorsement in hand did he look outward for ways to reinforce his policy through international cooperation. He then discovered a new and gratifying willingness on the part of other governments to take U.S. macroeconomic proposals and preferences seriously. At a meeting of G-7 finance ministers the normal resistance of foreign

26. One rationale for Clinton's inward-first approach was later provided by Theodore H. Moran, who was to become a senior adviser to the policy planning staff in Clinton's State Department: "Since 1980 the United States has consumed almost $1.5 trillion more than it has produced, while two of the prospective 'challengers' alone, the Germans and the Japanese, have accumulated more than $1 trillion in future demands on our assets. Reversing this Paul Kennedy-esque trend would strengthen U.S. freedom of action (present and future) in comparison to an America becoming more indebted to or owned by foreigners. It would foster external respect, rather than creeping contempt. But it cannot be accomplished by external assertiveness. It can only be accomplished by altering our internal consumption/savings ratio" (1993, p. 212).

governments to U.S. leadership was replaced by respect and deference. As U.S. Treasury Secretary Lloyd Bentsen explained, "Fortunately, we were able to bring to the table something that the Group of Seven countries had been admonishing us about for some time, and that was getting our own house in order. So we have been in a position to help restore some leadership."[27]

Clinton's inward-first approach to macroeconomic policy leadership also led to greater harmony at the Group of Seven economic summit in Tokyo in July 1993. On the eve of that meeting the U.S. Senate joined the House in passing (by one vote) a detailed version of the president's domestic deficit reduction plan. Thus Clinton was able to go outward with considerable credibility. "For the first time in a very long time," he announced, "an American president can go to a meeting of the G-7 nations in a position of economic strength."[28] At the Tokyo meeting Clinton won explicit praise from the G-7 leaders for his "long overdue" budget-cutting efforts. Japan then accepted the need for more stimulus policies of its own by signing a communiqué which stated that its growth should be driven by "strong domestic demand."

Clinton also came away from that meeting with a new framework for a U.S.-Japanese trade agreement, which committed Japan to a significant decrease in its current account surplus on the condition that the United States continue to pursue medium-term budget deficit reduction. U.S. officials defended this unusual linkage not only for its effect (which proved to be overstated) on trade policy attitudes in Japan, but also for its incentive to Congress to press for more deficit reduction. Upon his return from the summit, Clinton was thus quick to turn the process inward again: "This certainly ought to strengthen the resolve of Congress. . . . There's no question that the other countries were very much encouraged by the determination of the United States to reduce its deficit, that they believe that's one of the things that has distorted the world economy for the last several years. And likewise, there is no question that some of our job growth we're going to have to do on our

---

27. Steven Greenhouse, "Nations Join on Economy," *New York Times*, May 2, 1993, p. 7.
28. Nancy Dunne, "U.S. Senate Passes Budget Cuts Plan," *Financial Times*, June 26-June 27, 1993, p. 3.

own. . . . I am hoping that what happened this week will strengthen the resolve of the Congress to go ahead and pass the economic plan."[29]

Having started the two-level game by asking for fiscal policy discipline at home, which strengthened his hand later to ask for cooperation abroad, Clinton was now using the cooperation he had secured abroad to firm up discipline at home. In this fashion he strengthened relationships of mutual accountability in all directions. Whereas the outward-first initiatives of his predecessors had weakened U.S. fiscal accountability both at home and abroad, Clinton's inward-first alternative produced significant results. Treasury Undersecretary Lawrence Summers later noted that the United States could now "stand out for [its] fiscal virtue rather than [its] fiscal sin in G-7 meetings."[30] At the 1994 economic summit, in Naples, Clinton bragged that "shrinking our budget deficit from the biggest among these nations to one of the smallest gives us the authority to speak and the credibility to be heard on the matters of discussion here."[31]

The budget plan enacted by Congress in August 1993 was only a small step toward restoring U.S. fiscal policy discipline. It was dismissed by some for its failure to raise middle-class taxes and to reduce significantly middle-class entitlements.[32] Even supporters of the plan admitted that it would only slow what was still an excessively rapid accumulation of government debt. Yet Clinton had done more to restore fiscal discipline with an inward-first approach than his immediate predecessors had done with the outward-first alternative.

Agricultural Policy

An outward-first approach might seem logically suited to agricultural policy reform because the reform problems are similar

---

29. "Clinton on Tokyo Conference: 'We Have Made a Serious Start'," *New York Times*, July 10, 1993, p. 5.

30. Summers implicitly rejected the outward-first approach, saying that "we didn't think it made sense to try to pull rabbits out of hats at G-7 meetings." See David Wessel, "Treasury Official Praises 'Fiscal Virtue' of the U.S., Suggests Others Follow Suit," *Wall Street Journal*, March 11, 1994, p. A2.

31. "Summit in Naples: . . . Tricky Day for the Dollar," *New York Times*, July 9, 1994, p. 4.

32. See Peterson (1993).

throughout the industrial world and unilateral reforms within one country can produce disadvantages for the farmers of that country. Moreover, inward-first reform of agricultural policy has failed in the past. In 1985, when the Reagan administration proposed sharp unilateral reductions in U.S. farm income supports at the depths of a financial crisis for farmers, Congress pronounced this proposal dead on arrival.[33] Yet the outward-first approach can falter as well.

The reform of agricultural policy is a long-standing political issue throughout most of the industrial world, where governments have engaged in the distortion of their internal agricultural commodity markets, often by fixing prices well above market-clearing levels for the benefit of politically well-organized agricultural lobbies. The level at which internal prices have been fixed has varied from one country to another, depending on the relative disadvantage of a country's agricultural sector to its industrial sector. In nations such as Germany and Japan, where agricultural resources are poor compared to those of industry, policymakers have fixed internal farm commodity prices high; in nations such as Australia or Canada, and to some extent the United States, where agricultural resources are relatively good, policymakers have propped up internal farm prices to a lesser degree. Economists Kym Anderson and Yujiro Hayami have explained 60 to 70 percent of all variation in nominal rates of farm sector protection, country by country, by reference to various indicators of comparative advantage of industrial sectors within countries.[34]

Such national farm policies do a poor job of protecting small- and middle-sized farmers because most of the benefits go to the largest farmers. Yet it is usually the waxing and waning budget cost of these policies, rather than their inequity, that drives reform processes. When international free market commodity prices fall as a result of global macroeconomic contraction, the budget costs of domestic farm policies can suddenly increase in all industrial countries at the same time.

This is what happened when global commodity prices slumped in the mid-1980s. Between the early years of that decade and

33. See Rapp (1988, p. 41).
34. See Anderson and Hayami (1986).

1986, the budget cost of U.S. farm programs increased to $26 billion (roughly a fivefold increase) and the budget cost of European Union farm subsidies and support measures roughly doubled, to $23 billion.[35] Political leaders in the United States and the European Union at that point began looking for ways to reduce the budget burdens implied by their generous internal farm supports.

When President Reagan's inward-first approach was pronounced dead on arrival by Congress in 1985, policy reform advocates in the United States opted for the outward-first alternative. The logic of internationalizing the issue seemed impeccable. Not only were the governments of all industrial countries simultaneously facing internal farm budget pressures; the farm support policies of these governments also interacted enough, through international commodity markets, to place political burdens on any one government that dared to initiate reform alone. The pain to each nation's farming sector if all nations reformed at the same time would thus be measurably less than the pain from an inward-first or unilateral reform that was not reciprocated abroad.[36]

Such thinking, as well as demands for trade liberalization from commodity exporters in developing countries, inspired a U.S. decision to seek agricultural policy reform primarily through the Uruguay Round of GATT negotiations, which in 1986 was getting under way. President Reagan explained that "no nation can unilaterally abandon current policies without being devastated by the policies of other countries. The only hope is for a major international agreement that commits everyone to the same actions and timetable."[37] Daniel G. Amstutz, the undersecretary of agriculture for international affairs and commodity programs, argued that "we must reject the 'go it alone' approach, and move toward a global

35. See Paarlberg (1988, p. 4).
36. The U.S. Department of Agriculture calculated, on the basis of world commodity prices in 1986–87, that the pain to U.S. farmers of an international liberalization of farm supports, in which all industrial countries participated, would have been roughly 38 percent less than the pain of a unilateral liberalization by the United States. Farmers in the European Union could have expected a 32 percent pain reduction benefit from simultaneous international action. See Roningen and Dixit (1989, pp. 25, 28).
37. See Rapp (1988, p. 150).

solution. The new round of trade negotiations is a major opportunity for making that move. . . [T]he international bargaining table is where the solution lies."[38]

The modest agricultural agreement that was reached in the Uruguay Round in December 1993, after seven years of effort, fell short of vindicating hope that significant farm policy reforms could be secured through international negotiation. In the United States, the European Union, and Japan the final Uruguay Round agreement did little more than give formal recognition to reforms already undertaken country-by-country. In the case of the United States and the European Community, the negotiations sometimes even proved an impediment to achieving unilateral reforms.[39]

The outward-first approach to agricultural policy reform faltered in GATT partly for the same reasons that macroeconomic policy coordination was faltering in the Group of Seven. Attempts to begin a reform process by negotiating with governments abroad raised complex new issues of international burden sharing, which then were manipulated by domestic opposition groups that preferred inaction. Some antireform groups were thus strengthened tactically by internationalization of the issue.

In the United States, government officials failed to anticipate the extent to which domestic farm lobbies opposed to reform could gain tactically by manipulating the GATT negotiations. Reformers in the United States had hoped the international negotiation process would diminish the influence of domestic farm lobbies by taking effective control over agricultural policy out of the hands of Congress and giving the initiative to trade policy officials in the executive branch. Reformers also hoped that once trade officials had struck a preemptive bargain with the European

38. Letter from Daniel G. Amstutz, U.S. Department of Agriculture, published in *Choices* (Fourth Quarter, 1986), p. 38.

39. Only in the case of some smaller countries, such as South Korea, did the terms of the international agreement go substantially beyond agricultural reforms that might have been undertaken anyway. South Korea's president Kim Young Sam used the agreement as an excuse to open the domestic rice market to imports. In a televised address in December 1993 he told South Koreans that "we are on the verge of being isolated from the world. Accordingly, we have no choice but to adopt this critical position." Quoted in Asra Q. Nomani and Bhushan Bahree, "GATT Teams Push Final Efforts to Set Global Trade Pacts as Deadline Looms," *Wall Street Journal*, December 19, 1993, p. A3.

Union and Japan and had built this bargain into a larger Uruguay Round package that included nonfarm as well as farm issues, it would be too late for domestic agricultural lobbies to resist.

In the United States farm lobbies scored their first tactical success in 1987 when the Reagan administration offered, as its opening position in the GATT agricultural negotiations, what came to be called the zero option—an extreme proposal to eliminate in ten years all farm supports that tended to distort production or trade. Farm lobbies in the United States knew that this proposal would prove so unacceptable to the European Union and Japan that it would deadlock the negotiation, so some of the most protectionist U.S. farm lobbies (including the sugar and dairy lobbies) endorsed the zero option and warned that they would settle for nothing less. When the U.S. trade representative, Clayton Yeutter, tried to back away from the zero option to avoid a deadlock at the Mid-Term Review Conference for the Uruguay Round in Montreal in December 1988, the U.S. farm lobby's tactic prevented him from doing so and the conference broke up without achievement.[40]

When the Bush administration backed away from the paralyzing zero option in 1989, U.S. farm lobbyists found other ways to manipulate the international negotiations to their own advantage. They adopted the outward-looking metaphor of arms control policy and argued that they should not have to accept domestic subsidy cuts while the international talks were under way because to do so would constitute unilateral disarmament and weaken the hand of U.S. GATT negotiators.[41] In 1989 the chair of the Senate Agriculture Committee, Patrick Leahy, rejected a proposed $2 billion reduction in U.S. farm subsidies by representing it as a giveaway of bargaining leverage in GATT: "If that is not telegraphing unilateral disarmament I do not know what is," Leahy said.[42]

The domestic farm lobby also began to demand more subsidies for use as bargaining chips, to be traded away to win a better deal

40. See Paarlberg (1992a, p. 36).

41 President Reagan invited this tactic when he labeled his negotiating position the zero option, a label borrowed from nuclear arms reduction talks in Europe.

42. Quoted in *Inside U.S. Trade*, February 3, 1989, p. 18.

in the international negotiations.[43] This tactic was used effectively in 1990 to pressure the Agriculture Department into accepting a marketing loan subsidy program for soybeans. It was also used effectively on numerous occasions to justify continuation of the so-called Export Enhancement Program (EEP), an export subsidy program originally justified as a response to EU export subsidies, yet one that angered Canada and Australia more than it pressured the EU.[44] By 1993, on the same dubious grounds of preserving negotiating credibility, farm groups had pressured the U.S. government into using EEP subsidies directly against Canada, a Uruguay Round ally.

It did not take long for agricultural lobbies in other countries to adopt similar manipulative tactics. In 1989–90 farm organizations in the European Union rejected internal commodity price cuts that had been recommended by the EU Commission, arguing that they should not be expected to sacrifice "without reciprocal measures taken by our GATT partners."[45] Farmers in France suggested that reform of the European Union's Common Agricultural Policy (CAP) was being imposed from the outside, by the Americans, and for that reason should be resisted. Rather than serving as an efficient means to reduce farm subsidies, the international negotiation thus began serving as an excuse for continuing or increasing farm supports.

Perhaps the most inventive manipulation of the international negotiations came in the fall of 1990, when U.S. farm lobbies attached to the final domestic budget reconciliation bill a so-called GATT-trigger provision, which was designed to oblige the secretary of agriculture to offer a range of new subsidies in the event of a failed Uruguay Round negotiation. These subsidies would include an additional $1 billion for export subsidies, a marketing loan for wheat and feed grains, a waiver on all acreage planting restrictions, and a reversal of part or all of the domestic budget

43. The arm-in-order-to-disarm tactic is unfortunate enough when it develops during an arms control negotiation; it has even less legitimacy in an agricultural reform, because most of the damage done by farm subsidies affects consumers and taxpayers at home rather than foreigners abroad. The problem of getting rid of farm subsidies is much closer to the problem of domestic gun control than to that of international arms control.

44. See Paarlberg (1990).

45. See U.S. Department of Agriculture (1989, p. 8).

cuts that had just been imposed unilaterally on the farm sector.[46] The Uruguay Round was originally supposed to have been completed at a ministerial conference in Brussels in December 1990, but that conference adjourned without result because of continuing differences between the United States and the European Union over agriculture. The United States had gone to the conference demanding a 75 percent reduction in aggregate measures of internal farm support over ten years, together with a 90 percent reduction in export subsidies; the European Union, with the backing of Japan, offered only an imprecise 30 percent overall support level reduction. When the conference deadlocked, President Bush, with his fast-track authority soon to expire, was forced to compensate the U.S. farm lobby with still more export subsidies to keep the negotiations going. In March 1991 he agreed to nearly double the farm export subsidy budget in fiscal year 1991—a $475 million increase.

Fortunately, while the outward-first strategy of reforming farm policy through GATT was faltering, a more traditional inward-first path to reform was being reopened by new domestic budget pressures. In the United States in the fall of 1990, a tumultuous struggle between the president and Congress over the Omnibus Budget Reconciliation Act resulted in a significant unilateral reform of U.S. domestic agricultural policies. The agricultural committees of Congress had originally intended to write a new farm bill in 1990 that would have enlarged U.S. farm supports, but the extraordinary budget crisis gave effective custody of the legislative process to the budget committees, and one result was a decision to cut U.S. domestic farm commodity programs unilaterally by a significant 25 percent over five years.[47] This action was so driven by domestic budget pressures that farm lobby complaints about the dangers of losing bargaining leverage in GATT were to no avail.

Almost at the same time reintensification of budget pressures forced the European Union Commission to adopt a parallel unilateral reform initiative. Farm support spending in the European Union had fallen in 1989 and 1990, but then increased sharply in 1991 (it rose by 26 percent in a year), helping to inspire a new

46. See Epstein and Ek (1992).
47. See Ek and Hanrahan (1991, p. 1).

policy reform plan. This was the so-called MacSharry Plan (named for agricultural commissioner Ray MacSharry), which called for roughly a 35 percent reduction in CAP commodity price guarantees over a three-year period. This inward-looking proposal implied a pace of EU agricultural reform that would be faster than the ten-year, 75 percent cut in support levels (just one component of prices) that had recently been demanded by the United States in the GATT negotiations. Like the earlier U.S. farm subsidy cuts, these European Union cuts were almost entirely inward-looking; when the EU Commission submitted its approved reform plan in August 1991, it did so without referring to the continuing GATT negotiations.

Only after budget-driven farm subsidy cuts had been taken unilaterally in the United States and the European Union did an opportunity arise to complete the agricultural part of Uruguay Round. This was done by redrafting the language of the multilateral agreement to reflect what had already been accomplished unilaterally. The resulting draft agreement by GATT director general Arthur Dunkel (the Dunkel draft), which called for a 20 to 36 percent support level reduction over a six-year period, took care to use a 1986–88 reference base, which meant that both the United States and the European Union would get full credit in GATT's calculations for what they had already unilaterally done outside of GATT. When the U.S. Department of Agriculture later studied the subsidy cut requirements of the Dunkel draft, it found that the EU would be able to meet a 20 percent cut in internal supports with no change at all in its current policies, and that in fourteen out of seventeen farm commodity areas the policies of the United States were already in full compliance with the projected reforms.[48]

No criticism is intended here of the use of an international agreement to lock in what had already been accomplished unilaterally. This is precisely the sequence of events that an inward-first strategy would prescribe. Building the terms of a prior domestic reform into a subsequent international agreement can enhance the

48. See U.S. Department of Agriculture (1993, p. 47) and U.S. Department of Agriculture (1992).

durability of an otherwise reversible unilateral reform. Such a sequence can be of considerable value in the agricultural policy area, because support levels tend to rise the minute budget pressures are relaxed.

Where the Dunkel draft did try to go beyond what had already been undertaken unilaterally, it only served to prolong the negotiating deadlock. Dunkel called for a 24 percent cut (over six years) in the volume of farm goods exported under subsidy, a cut that implied some significant new policy disciplines in the European Union. The MacSharry reform plan had provided strong implicit assurances that subsidized EU exports would eventually fall (by removing the production stimulus of high prices and by calling for acreage reductions), but it had contained no explicit reduction guarantees. The government of France was therefore angered, in November 1992, when EU Commission negotiators, in discussions with the United States at Blair House, agreed to accept a 21 percent cut in subsidized export tonnage. The United States thought it was making the concession, because a 24 percent cut was called for in the Dunkel draft, but to the French the cut accepted at Blair House was unacceptable because it went beyond the explicit terms of the agricultural policy reforms agreed upon within the European Union. The government of France argued that the EU Commission had no authority to concede anything in GATT negotiations that went beyond the terms of the prior internal CAP reform, and then deadlocked the negotiations for another year by threatening a veto.[49]

As long as the United States refused to reconsider the terms of the Blair House agreement on export subsidy restraints, negotiations remained at a standstill. It was not until late in 1993, when the Clinton administration yielded on several important parts of the Blair House formula (the administration was confronting expiration of fast-track authority) that the deadlock broke. The United States agreed to a slower initial pace for reducing subsidized exports and accepted an extended peace clause that would restrict U.S. options to initiate formal challenges to the European Union's

---

49. The reactions of French farmers played a role in this decision. A protest of three thousand farmers in the streets of Paris, against the Blair House agreement, degenerated into a stone and bottle throwing clash in which fifty police officers were injured.

agricultural policies. To bring Japan into the final agricultural agreement, the United States also dropped its long-standing demand for an immediate conversion of Japan's rice import restrictions to tariffs.[50] When the United States agreed to give Japan at least a six-year period in which to delay tariffication of its rice market, the terms of the Uruguay Round agricultural deal had been diluted enough to provide a basis for agreement on all three sides.

How significant was the agricultural component of the final Uruguay Round package? A report by the National Center for Food and Agricultural Policy observes that "essentially, the Agreement does little more than ratify the recent unilateral reforms in the EC, the U.S., Canada, and Japan . . . and will, therefore, barely make a dent in the cost of farm support to OECD [Organization for Economic Cooperation and Development] consumers and taxpayers."[51] Any internationally negotiated reform of agricultural policy, however small, is to be cheered. The point here is that reform agreements proved essentially unreachable abroad until both the United States and the European Union had undertaken most of the reforms in question unilaterally at home.

Global Environmental Policy

Environmental policy is a third area in which inward-first leadership options will be attractive for the United States in the years ahead. This might seem surprising, given the perception by many that global environmental problems require global solutions. Vice President Albert Gore, before entering office, proposed annual environmental summit meetings among heads of state, similar to the annual economic summits but involving leaders of poor countries as well as rich countries. According to Gore, "there is only one answer: we must negotiate international agreements that establish global constraints on acceptable behavior."[52]

50. Japan began to open its domestic rice market to imports unilaterally in 1993 after bad weather had produced an unusually small domestic crop, yet it continued to resist a key U.S. demand to convert all nontariff restrictions to tariffs.

51. See Sanderson (1994, p. 2).

52. See Gore (1993, p. 302).

Such outward-oriented arguments place too much faith in the ability of the U.S. political system to offer stable and coherent positions on environmental questions to the rest of the world. U.S. policymaking on environmental issues is so penetrated by clashing interest groups and partisans that inward-first action is probably necessary before the United States can help to build an international consensus on environmental solutions.

Coherent outward-first leadership by the United States on environmental policy is difficult because the nation's institutional processes for making environmental policy are among those least insulated from private sector and interest group activism and from domestic partisan differences. Such public penetration of the policy process was evident during the Bush and Quayle administration in the operation of the Competitiveness Council, a cabinet-level body that allowed private companies unhappy with environmental regulations to seek redress at the political level. President Clinton abolished the council after taking office, but created instead a White House Office on Environmental Policy that ensured environmental activists a parallel means to end-run the normal policy process.

Domestic laws and legal processes also constrain environmental policy. Examples already mentioned include the U.S. court decision in 1990 that overrode the Bush administration's policy on Mexican tuna fishing practices and the court ruling in 1993 that threatened to delay President Clinton's pursuit of a NAFTA agreement with Mexico by calling for preparation of an environmental impact statement on the treaty. The mere possibility of domestic litigation can discourage U.S. entry into international environmental agreements. Not wishing to be taken to court, the U.S. government tends to avoid formal environmental commitments abroad.

State and local governments are also exceptionally powerful in U.S. environmental policymaking. As many as 700 toxic air pollutants were recently being regulated by state and local agencies in the United States, compared with just 7 such pollutants regulated at the federal level by the Environmental Protection Agency (EPA).[53] The dominance of state and local government in environmental

---

53. *Environment Reporter*, May 4, 1990, p. 124.

regulation increased during the first half of the 1980s when the antiregulatory attitudes of the Reagan administration blocked environmental activism at the federal level. Even when sympathetic Democrats are in the White House, local regulatory jurisdictions may be jealously guarded. In the NAFTA debate in 1993, the states extracted a promise from U.S. trade negotiators that the supplemental environmental accord with Mexico not be used by private legal challengers to preempt state or local laws. At the same time, however, environmentalists in the United States were making no secret of their intent to use the supplemental agreement to compel changes in Mexico's legal procedures.

These features of the environmental policy process in the United States often complicate the presentation of a single outward-looking face to the rest of the world. Consider the performance of the U.S. government at the time of the United Nations earth summit conference in Rio de Janeiro in 1992. The Competitiveness Council had helped to persuade President Bush to adopt a skeptical view toward the conference and to resist firm legal commitments on climate change and biodiversity. During the conference the head of the U.S. delegation, EPA administrator William K. Reilly, urged President Bush in a confidential message to reverse his position and support the treaty on biodiversity, but to no avail when the message was almost immediately leaked to the press. On the other hand, visiting U.S. representatives and senators used the conference to engage in openly partisan criticism of the official U.S. position and of their own president. Tommy Koh of Singapore, chair of the conference's main working session, was later heard to remark that "this will teach the United Nations not to hold a conference in an American election year."[54]

The fractious and participatory U.S. policy process may be bad for environmental policy coordination abroad, but it has a good record in terms of environmental policy content at home. When President Bush spoke at the earth summit in 1992, he could correctly assert that the United States had "the world's tightest air-quality standards on cars and factories, the most advanced laws for protecting lands and waters, and the most open processes for

54. "Lessons of Rio," *New York Times,* June 14, 1992, p. 10.

public participation [in the making of environmental policy]."[55] According to the Organization for Economic Cooperation and Development, the United States spends a greater proportion of its GNP on environmental controls than any other nation in the developed world. Because of tighter restrictions contained in the 1990 Clean Air Act, the Environmental Protection Agency has estimated this proportion will increase from 1.7 percent in 1990 to 3.0 percent by the end of the century.[56] Other OECD countries may have developed more orderly and consensual ways of making environmental policy, but in such countries (Japan is the prime example) the content of environmental policy is typically weaker than in the United States.[57]

Given the distinctive U.S. policymaking process, there are good reasons for the United States to lead with tough inward-first policies at home, whether or not other nations are yet ready to promise reciprocal action. An inward-first approach could lead in the short run to stronger domestic environmental policies, and in the long run to stronger international environmental agreements. The United States could demonstrate the feasibility and affordability of new policy instruments and stimulate timely investment in substitute technologies and industrial processes, and hence widen the path for pursuing international agreements.

Even the Montreal Protocol of 1987 on stratospheric ozone protection, an agreement often cited as a model of outward-oriented U.S. leadership, was actually built on an important inward-first foundation. The United States was able to get other countries to agree to reduce chlorofluorocarbon (CFC) production in part because of its own prior willingness to reduce CFC production at home. The first U.S. leadership step on this issue was a unilateral domestic ban on CFCs in aerosol sprays, enacted by Congress in 1977 as an amendment to the Clean Air Act in response to pressures by domestic

55. "The Earth Summit," New York Times, June 13, 1992, p. 5.
56. See Paarlberg (1992b, p. 225).
57. See Pharr and Badaracco (1986). For a concise comparative review of environmental policymaking institutions and procedures in the United States, Japan, and the European Union, see Vernon (1993).

environmental groups.[58] The benefits of this step were considerable: in addition to reduced CFC production (U.S. production fell by half, which implied a 25 percent fall in world production), private companies such as DuPont began to invest in the development of ozone-safe CFC substitutes.

The United States was well positioned to take the lead in reducing CFCs because half of the world's production was still in the United States in the late 1970s and because the costs to the U.S. economy of reducing CFC production would be relatively small compared with the projected gain. The total cost to the U.S. economy of the Montreal Protocol controls on CFCs, as estimated by the Environmental Protection Agency in 1988, was $27 billion, whereas the estimated benefit was $6.4 trillion, mostly in the form of avoided cancer deaths in the U.S. population born before 2075.[59] Rather than discouraging parallel actions abroad, this unilateral U.S. initiative coincided with the creation, by the United Nations Environment Programme, of the international Coordinating Committee on the Ozone Layer, a model for the more ambitious international regulatory efforts of the 1980s.

After a period of regression during the first Reagan administration, when federal environmental activism diminished, the international regulation of ozone moved ahead in November 1986 when the U.S. government formally embraced the concept of an immediate international freeze on CFC use, followed by phased reductions essentially to zero. This international thrust also had important domestic foundations. In March 1986 DuPont had announced that substitutes for CFCs could be available within five years if market conditions and policies warranted the development effort, and in September 1986 a coalition of U.S. industries issued a policy statement supporting international regulation of CFCs.[60] The subsequent outward-looking negotiation was thus in part an attempt to generalize to the rest of the industrial world (and especially to Europe) a regulatory policy already acceptable

58. See Benedick (1991, p. 23). Even before this step, individual states had taken action against aerosol sprays and U.S. consumers had reduced their purchases of such sprays by nearly two-thirds out of concern about the environment.

59. See Parson (1993, p. 69).

60. Parson (1993, p. 41); Benedick (1991, p. 32).

to industry in the United States. This was not a case of using a prior international agreement to preempt domestic political or industry opposition in a two-level game, because by 1986 there was no longer significant opposition of that kind at home.

Richard Benedick, the principal U.S. negotiator of the Montreal Protocol, subsequently concluded that "it may be desirable for a leading country or group of countries to take preemptive environmental protection measures in advance of a global agreement." Benedick endorsed this approach because he saw that unilateral actions can serve as examples that legitimate change, make moral suasion by leading countries credible, slow adverse trends (thus buying time for future negotiations and technical solutions), and stimulate research into those solutions.[61]

What does the Montreal Protocol experience suggest for U.S. leadership options in other global environmental issues, such as biodiversity and climate change? In regard to biodiversity, one lesson has been the importance of building unity at home before attempting to lead abroad. President Bush was heavily criticized for not signing the biodiversity treaty at the earth summit conference in June 1992, yet he lacked the domestic political leeway to do so, given the views of most U.S. biotechnology and pharmaceutical companies at the time. Even President Clinton, a strong treaty supporter, recognized the danger in preempting powerful domestic actors with an international agreement. In 1993, before formally announcing his intent to sign the treaty, Clinton consulted with U.S. firms and agreed to attach to it an interpretive statement that would secure patent protections and opportunities to pursue research and innovation.[62] A few environmental organizations criticized this approach as a compromise that undercut the international regulatory effort, but Clinton opted for putting domestic consensus building first, knowing that he would need a two-thirds vote in the Senate to ratify the treaty. A treaty without support from U.S. industry would in any case be ineffective.

---

61. Benedick (1991, p. 206).
62. Understandings to this effect, crafted by the State Department, were later incorporated into Clinton's November 16, 1993, Letter of Submittal to the Senate.

On the issue of global warming Clinton also decided to put domestic consensus building first, albeit with less success. He had pledged during the 1992 campaign to limit U.S. carbon dioxide (CO_2) emissions to 1990 levels by the year 2000.[63] By setting a specific date for achieving specific emissions reductions this pledge went beyond the watered-down terms Bush had imposed on the Framework Convention on Climate Change negotiated at the earth summit conference. The quickest way to reduce greenhouse gas emissions, including CO_2, would be through a broadly based energy tax, yet once in office Clinton discovered how little domestic political support there would be for such a measure. At the initiative of Vice President Gore, Clinton's original budget proposal included a broad-based energy tax designed to reduce the budget deficit and discourage fossil fuel consumption. This tax was rejected by Congress and replaced with an environmentally insignificant 4.3-cent-a-gallon increase in the 14.1-cent federal tax on gasoline. Even Gore was forced to admit a lack of consensus in Congress to support a broad-based energy tax.[64]

An inward-first approach to energy taxes thus for the moment failed. Would an outward-first approach have done any better? The outward-first option would have been to overcome domestic barriers by negotiating an international agreement that would move all industrial countries toward an energy tax at the same time.[65] The risks of going outward first would be congressional resistance during negotiations and thus being unable to negotiate credibly or meeting such resistance after the negotiation and not being able to deliver. Linking Clinton's entire first-year domestic economic package to a difficult international negotiation on energy taxes would also risk delaying enactment of the package.

When Clinton did unveil a climate change policy in October 1993, it did not envision an international agreement on energy

63. Clinton and Gore (1992, p. 97).

64. See Woodward (1994, pp. 221–22).

65. For an elaboration of this proposal, see Nelson and Rashish (1993). A special logic supported going international in this fashion, since the EU had proposed an energy tax of its own in 1992 but had then hesitated to act alone, fearing possible damage to the competitiveness of European industry.

taxes or even tightening the Framework Convention on Climate Change. Nor did Clinton take the inward-first step of tightening auto fuel efficiency standards even though he had pledged to do so in his 1992 campaign. Apparently wishing to avoid a new battle with Congress, Clinton announced the formation of two modest government-industry partnerships, to be run by the Department of Energy and EPA, known as Climate Challenge and Climate Wise Companies. These voluntary programs were designed to entice utilities and other U.S. companies into negotiating domestic emissions reduction agreements with the government (no international offsets would count) in return for a mix of technical assistance and public recognition, at a total cost to taxpayers of only $1.9 billion between 1994 and 2000.[66]

So modest was this approach, and so far was it from the vision of a bold, outward-first international leadership initiative, that it was criticized by environmental groups as a significant policy retreat. In April 1994 the Natural Resources Defense Council and other environmental groups charged that the Clinton plan would achieve only one-third of the emissions reductions it promised. But Clinton knew that he lacked a domestic consensus to support both a bolder policy and credible negotiations abroad. His policy promised at least to generate practical experience in the discovery of guidelines and criteria for estimating and monitoring greenhouse gas emissions reductions, which could later be valuable in negotiating a more ambitious global agreement.[67]

Given the reality of a divided and hesitant domestic political audience on climate change issues, more outward-looking leadership by the United States was probably impossible in 1993. The United States had been able to provide effective international leadership on the ozone issue partly because of its earlier success in acting first at home. In environmental policy as in farm policy and fiscal policy, trying to do for the world what has not been possible at home is a formula for trouble.

---

66. The Clinton plan also selected a more comprehensive benchmark for measuring progress—greenhouse gas emissions, rather than CO_2 emissions reductions.

67. See Clinton and Gore (1993), p. 4.

Conclusions

Issues of farm, fiscal, and environmental policy are not offered here as necessarily typical of the foreign economic policy problems that U.S. leaders will face in the years ahead. All three are behind-the-border issues in the sense that the relevant policy actions usually take place internally. Somewhat different lessons might be drawn by examining at-the-border issues such as trade policy and beyond-the-border issues such as the mining of the ocean floor or central bank interventions in foreign exchange markets. For these issues outward-first leadership might be the only appropriate approach for the United States, no matter how difficult. Because tomorrow's more deeply integrated world economy is likely to feature more frequent disputes and discussions over the coordination of behind-the-border issues, however, the lessons drawn here should have growing relevance.

Chapter 6

Leadership Abroad Begins at Home

*T*HE PRINCIPAL CONCLUSION to be drawn from this study is that leadership abroad may require prior efforts to move policy unilaterally at home. Outward-oriented leadership initiatives, when launched ahead of effective domestic policy change, or in lieu of domestic policy change, have not always produced the intended effect abroad, and at times have even undermined prospects for further change at home.

This is a conclusion about where good international leadership policy begins, not about where it ends. It is a conclusion about the value of acting inward *first,* not an endorsement of acting inward *only.* And it is certainly not an endorsement of protectionism or isolationism, because liberal internationalism often must be built on a firm inward-first foundation, as has been demonstrated.

For an inward-first approach to succeed, the domestic policies embraced unilaterally must be sound. Not all policies initiated at home will measure up to this standard (as in the case of U.S. fiscal policy in the 1980s and energy tax policy in 1993). Yet the cure for an unsound inward-first policy is usually a better inward-first policy rather than an outward-first coordination exercise or an attempted two-level game finesse.

Although inward-first leadership will not be easy for the United States in the years ahead, maintaining an effective outward-first leadership posture could be even more difficult. The relative economic dominance of the United States is now substantially diminished from what it was just after World War II; mature industrial

economies abroad have recovered from the war and younger industrial economies, especially in East Asia, are growing rapidly.
The end of the cold war has reduced deference to U.S. initiatives
in the international arena, and at the same time reduced the
political capacity of the United States to take such initiatives.

Because of these changed circumstances a number of long-
standing institutional constraints to outward-first leadership have
been unmasked. These constraints—divided government, congressional power over foreign economic policy, divisions and discontinuities within the executive branch, public participation in the
policy process, legalism in policymaking, the growing power of
state and local government, and an insular culture—were significantly muted during the cold war era.

Especially in today's more deeply integrated world economy,
these distinctive features of the U.S. political system make continuation of outward-first policy leadership more difficult. It was hard
enough for the U.S. political system, during the cold war era of
more shallow integration, to engage in coherent outward-first leadership. Today's markets require harmonization and coordination of
policies behind the border. The policies required will engage all of
the fragmented and most inward-looking components of the U.S.
political system, and thus would be difficult to coordinate in an
outward-first fashion.

In pursuing leadership abroad, the United States should therefore
reverse the order in which internal and external policy initiatives have
traditionally been taken. Rather than starting abroad first, with initiatives pointed toward preemptive international bargains or agreements, the United States should more often start at home with
initiatives pointed at internal problems, and especially at the internal
sources of international imbalances. Even where the domestic political system of the United States has traditionally been weakened by
lack of discipline (as in fiscal policy) or by social division and sectoral
conflict (as in agricultural policy and environmental policy), leadership abroad must begin at home. Outward-looking efforts will stand
little chance of being consistent or credible abroad until unity of
purpose has been achieved or restored at home.

Outward-looking policy coordination with other governments
remains important, but should more often be undertaken as a

second step. If a fragmented and self-absorbed United States attempts to lead abroad without having first overcome its differences and divisions at home, it will not only send confusing signals to foreign governments, but will risk further loss of discipline and accountability in its domestic policy debate. In theory perhaps, the political will to solve problems at home could be strengthened by prior efforts to ensure complementary or parallel policy actions by others abroad. The links of accountability in the U.S. political system are already so weak, however, that internationalizing a policy issue might give domestic opponents of change another excuse for inaction. Domestic opponents of reform can point to the uncertain or inadequate contributions of foreigners as a reason to withhold their own contributions.

The internal policy debate often produces better results if confined to what the U.S. government can do without prior assurance of foreign cooperation. Once the first step has been taken at home, foreign cooperation can become easier to secure. In the examples reviewed here, unilateral fiscal policy discipline was the best way to increase subsequent cooperation within the Group of Seven; unilateral agricultural policy reform was key to the completion of a GATT agreement on farm trade; and unilateral CFC reductions substantially widened the path toward the Montreal Protocol.

Once the United States has moved to put its own house in order, it is better positioned to go abroad in search of cooperative followers. If U.S. policymakers look abroad before taking sufficient measures at home—perhaps in hope of using an international agreement to finesse domestic political opposition, or because negotiating with foreign counterparts is more pleasant than negotiating with partisan domestic opponents and congressional committee chairs—they are likely to embarrass themselves in both settings.

Unsound inward-first actions could impose negative spillovers on rest of the world economy, but that is also a danger with outward-first actions. In the post–cold war era, the tradition of sharing or lifting international burdens could be replaced by a less generous habit of burden shifting. If that happens, an outward-first leadership approach could degenerate into nonproductive squabbling over relative contributions and relative gains.

Today the inward-first approach is more likely to generate positive spillovers. If the United States disciplines fiscal policy at home, in its own self-interest, it will help rather than harm the prospects for long-term growth in other countries. If the United States reduces its internal farm support levels unilaterally, it will not only help consumers and taxpayers at home, but also reduce distortions in international commodity markets. If the United States moves unilaterally to reduce CFC or greenhouse gas emissions, it will help rather than harm others.

So likely is the inward-first approach to lead to positive spillovers that it might be criticized for being too generous rather than too selfish. Yet such a danger is also overstated, especially in regard to behind-the-border actions. Internally driven political calculations will dominate behind-the-border issues in other countries just as in the United States. Thus there will be less opportunity for the international strategizing that can tempt a nation into free riding or defection. An example of strong and successful policy action set by the United States could just as easily heighten internal political pressures abroad to follow the U.S. lead.

In the cold war era, leadership by the United States was founded upon strategic interactions among governments in pursuit of a shared security objective and often required outward-first action. With the passing of the cold war a more diffuse pattern of inward-first actions will become the better way to lead. Even some of the original cold-war warriors are coming around to this point of view. George F. Kennan, celebrating his ninetieth birthday in 1994, argued that it was now time for American political leaders to "look closely at our own society" and to remember that "it is primarily by example, never by precept, that a country such as ours exerts the most useful influence beyond its borders."[1]

---

1. Remarks by George F. Kennan at the New York Council on Foreign Relations on the occasion of his ninetieth birthday, excerpted in *New York Times*, March 14, 1994, p. A17.

Comments

Jeffry A. Frieden

The future of international economic integration depends on the future of American foreign and domestic economic policy. Robert Paarlberg's essay appraises current trends in American policy and recommends how they might be guided in a constructive and positive manner. It presents an instructive survey of American political and policymaking institutions, and of America's changing position in the world. The essay comes to some compelling conclusions about the need for any potential leadership on the part of the United States—or participation in cooperative international ventures—to rest firmly on domestic political support.

Paarlberg's summary of the domestic setting within which American policy is made is comprehensive and largely convincing. His interpretation of the implications of the changing global context of American policy is also persuasive.

In these comments, as is customary, I emphasize dimensions the essay seems to me to underplay, as well as those few of Paarlberg's assertions with which I actually disagree. I found some of his categories and definitions opaque, and some of his descriptions incomplete. Most important is my broad concern that the essay does not adequately present and apply a clear method to analyze American foreign policymaking. This analytical gap makes it diffi-

Jeffry A. Frieden is professor of political science at the University of California, Los Angeles.

cult to evaluate some of Paarlberg's empirical conclusions and policy recommendations.

Paarlberg's Argument

The organizing principle of Paarlberg's monograph is the distinction between what he calls outward-first and inward-first foreign policies. By this he means to differentiate between an approach to foreign policy that emphasizes the making of international agreements and the pursuit of international objectives, on the one hand, and an approach that stresses the importance of the prior resolution of domestic policy problems, on the other hand.

Paarlberg argues that in the early postwar period, the United States was willing and able to act outward-first, partly because of international conditions, which allowed the United States extraordinary room to maneuver, and partly because of domestic circumstances that led to a strong consensus in favor of a particular sort of American foreign policies.

Paarlberg believes that over the past twenty years this sort of outward-first policymaking has become increasingly difficult to sustain. At the international level, the decline of America's relative economic position, the end of the cold war, and the galloping pace of global economic integration have reduced the ability of the United States to exert effective international leadership. Domestically, the national consensus over foreign policy has broken down, as illustrated by the decline of congressional deference on foreign policy.

Paarlberg details characteristics of the American political and social system that have long been obstacles to the exercise of outward-first leadership, including such features of American politics as a powerful Congress, a relatively weak executive, interest-group penetration of politics, and federalism. These enduring characteristics of American politics, Paarlberg argues, tend largely to impede outward-first leadership, and only the unusual conditions after World War II were able to overcome what might be regarded as a constitutional block to outward-first foreign policies.

Now, Paarlberg believes, the United States will and should revert to type, focusing on resolving domestic problems and only later moving on to global policy issues. Unless the domestic front is secured, Paarlberg asserts, American international initiatives will be unsuccessful, and the domestic front can only be secured by giving it priority in the formulation of policy.

The argument is clear and coherent. I think that very few analysts would disagree with the general tenor of Paarlberg's essay, that America's international position depends on domestic support for this position and the national ability to make good on global commitments.

However, the essay suffers from two weaknesses that undermine the force of Paarlberg's argument. First, the very categories Paarlberg uses may be more confusing than illuminating. Second, and more fundamental, Paarlberg's assertions are not adequately supported by an analysis of the forces underlying the making of American foreign policy. To truly evaluate Paarlberg's views, a more complete picture of both their logic and their analytical implications is needed. As it stands, the essay appears to be a brief for a particular position rather than an analysis whose conclusions lead to a set of policy implications.

Definitions and Related Matters

Paarlberg frames the issue in a way that may obscure more than it clarifies, for the distinction between "outward-first" and "inward-first" policies is labored. Even the definition of the terms seems fluid. At the outset Paarlberg associates them solely with chronological sequence, so that in the former policies are undertaken first abroad and in the latter first at home. However, over the course of the essay the terms appear to take on much broader significance. At times, for example, Paarlberg seems to identify the inward-first approach with unilateralism and the primacy of domestic concerns as well as with temporal sequence.

Running through the essay is Paarlberg's quite accurate sense of a common, enduring feature of American foreign policymaking—indeed, of the foreign policymaking of most countries. There is often a clash between pressures to undertake foreign actions and pressures to respond to domestic needs. This can express itself in domestic conflict that makes it difficult for governments to abide by international agreements (or to ratify them), in divisions in the national political arena between globally and nationally oriented groups, and in many other ways.

Important as this international-domestic divergence may be, I do not think that Paarlberg's version of the dichotomy captures the essence of the problem. For example, Paarlberg presents American foreign economic policy in the early postwar period as an example of something that is "outward-first." In his telling, the crucial consideration was that policies were formulated first in relationship to the country's international goals, after which Congress and other domestic actors acquiesced. I think that this is misleading; Congress and domestic groups were heavily involved in many aspects of foreign economic policy even in the 1950s, and successive administrations took congressional concerns into account in their international negotiations. It was hardly irrelevant that the immediate postwar Congress was dominated by a traditionally insular and protectionist Republican party; this fact fundamentally constrained the Truman administration. After all, the GATT had its origins in the administration's knowledge that it would be unable to obtain congressional approval of the International Trade Organization, even though this approval appeared at the time a crucial component of American postwar leadership.

Certainly American foreign economic policy in the 1940s and 1950s was different than it has been since 1970. What changed, however, was not the *sequence* of American trade policymaking, but the level and vehemence of domestic pressures for trade protection and export promotion, the shape of the global economy, and the geopolitical context in which policy was made. Paarlberg mentions all these factors in his discussion of the American experience; none of them seems to have much to do with whether policy was formulated inward-first or outward-first.

The executive, after all, would be foolish to pursue an international initiative requiring congressional approval without taking into account the position of Congress. In fact, some observers suggest that congressional supremacy in policymaking is so great that implicit threats of congressional action are enough to "discipline" the executive. I mention this view not necessarily to endorse it, only to illustrate that chronology is not priority, and that if the principal distinction between inward-first and outward-first policies is chronological, this is a classic distinction without a difference.

Although there is an important point here about the potential conflict between international and domestic goals, I do not find the inward- or outward-first distinction useful. It is not so much the sequence of policymaking that distinguishes the two poles of the dichotomy, but the relative weights attached to international and domestic factors by policymakers (and by analysts). I return to this point below.

Several other, more minor, matters also left me a bit dissatisfied. Paarlberg presents a series of domestic and international factors that he believes affect the ability of the United States to play a leadership role internationally. Virtually all of them are important, but the reasons for their expected impact on American policy are often obscure. Some of the factors are constants of American politics and American society—such as its federalist structure and general parochialism. Others, such as America's relative economic position in the world, have changed in important ways. Inasmuch as Paarlberg largely focuses on changes in American policy capabilities, it is not at all obvious what role the constants might have played in this—after all, the United States has been a federal system since its inception. It is also unclear what the precise impact of the changes has been, and on which aspects of American foreign policy.

These problems may simply be born of misunderstanding. But if one is to evaluate Paarlberg's analysis and recommendations, a better-articulated definition of his terms and of his analytical argument is needed. In this context, I turn to some of the problems I see in the way Paarlberg develops his analysis and recommendations.

Analytical Foundations

I found the logic of Paarlberg's analysis difficult to follow in spots. I also was not fully convinced by the evidence he brings to bear in support of his analysis. This response is largely because

Paarlberg moves rapidly from his definition of the issues to a strong statement of his policy recommendations—that the United States pursue an inward-first strategy—without spending enough time developing the analysis on which the recommendations are bases.

Even the most policy-oriented document rests on analytical principles, for recommendations for action depend on some causal notion of the impact these actions will have. To evaluate the efficacy and implications of such policy recommendations, indeed, their expected effects must be demonstrated. This can only be done on the basis of consistent analytical principles—an explanation of why the policies should have particular effects—and some empirical evidence that this causal relationship has in fact operated in practice. Without this process, policy recommendations are simply personal opinions.

Paarlberg makes a series of implicit analytical arguments in his essay. Some of them have to do with the effects of international conditions and American political institutions on American foreign policy. Others have to do with the anticipated impact of particular styles of policymaking (outward-first or inward-first) on the sustainability of American foreign policy. In all instances, there is presumably a logical case for the causal argument Paarlberg makes, but this case is rarely stated. For this reason, the very strong conclusions Paarlberg draws, in favor of an inward-first strategy, are difficult to evaluate in any more than an impressionistic way.

Changes in America's international position have certainly affected its foreign policy. Paarlberg details, among other things, that other countries' per capita incomes and overall output have risen relative to those of the United States, the persistence of low American savings and investment rates relative to those abroad, and America's large trade and budget deficits. But in many instances I did not see precisely how Paarlberg saw these developments affecting the making of American foreign policy more generally. His summary of the problems raises legitimate concerns, but it does not present a clear view of how and why they enter into analysis of the process and outcome of U.S. foreign policymaking.

By the same token, some of Paarlberg's assertions about the foreign-policy implications of American politics and institutions require firmer argumentation. For example, his notion that interest-group penetration, a weak executive, federalism, and divided government make external commitments difficult is plausible. However, it runs counter to the assertion of some political scientists that precisely because it is so difficult to achieve agreement among several political actors (the executive, Congress, the states, different parties, various interest groups), once agreement is reached, it is eminently credible to external interlocutors. A parliamentary regime can change policies with a simple change in government, goes this argument; much more continuity (and thus much more credibility) inheres to the American system. Whether Paarlberg is right or wrong is hard to evaluate, for he presents little logical or empirical foundation to his assertions along these lines.

And, despite the fact that the inward- or outward-first dichotomy is central to Paarlberg's argument, he does not present a clear general explanation of the causes and effects of the two strategies. The sequence of decisionmaking often makes a significant difference, given the possibility of agenda-setting and other first-mover advantages—whether in interstate negotiations or in bargaining between the president and Congress. However, the impact of sequencing varies widely across issue, time, and space: in some cases, being first to act is better, in others, acting second is better, in still others sequence makes little difference. Inasmuch as Paarlberg's principal point is about the need for domestic policy to be formulated first, he needs to present the reasoning that justifies this point.

All in all, I tend to agree with many of Paarlberg's conclusions, though largely because of the coincidence of our mutual predispositions. Paarlberg's argument would be more convincing if it were grounded in more firmly based analysis, brought to bear more systematically on the historical and contemporary evidence, and oriented toward showing how both analysis and evidence demonstrate the validity of his policy recommendations.

International and Domestic Constraints on
American Foreign Policy

Paarlberg's essay is a valuable contribution toward understanding the making of foreign policy in the context of growing global integration. But I believe that the issues he addresses can more fruitfully be analyzed—and policy implications drawn—if we focus not on an inward-outward dichotomy but rather on constraints that affect the incentives for policymakers to undertake particular policies.

Foreign policy is always made within constraints. These might include a populace unwilling to finance or serve in wars, a reduced fiscal base for foreign ventures, relative military weakness, or skeptical foreign investors. Such constraints are not straitjackets: policymakers have engaged in unpopular wars, financed foreign policy by extractive or inflationary means, attempted to sidestep superior opposing force, and ignored market pressures. But these constraints impose costs on policymakers. The more unpopular a foreign venture, the greater its domestic political cost; the more hostile foreign investors, the more difficult it may be to sustain economic growth, and presumably the greater the domestic political cost.

In evaluating the context within which policymakers operate, the distinction between international and domestic constraints is useful. All else equal, national politicians would like to pursue only foreign and domestic policies that improve the position of all their constituents, but this is usually impossible. Often policymakers are faced with a foreign policy prospect that they believe has significant benefits to the country, but will also impose significant costs. Conversely, politicians often understand that pursuing domestic goals may have both important national benefits and conflict with foreign-policy considerations. This leads to one sort of contradiction inherent in American foreign policymaking: between the domestic and international costs and benefits of national policies.

In a sense, the incentives of relevance to policymakers are all domestic, for politicians' tenure in office is normally the direct result of domestic politics (democratic or otherwise). But this reality does not lessen the potential international-domestic divide.

Some domestic constituencies may value internationally oriented policy very highly: firms with overseas interests, immigrant groups with ties to their home countries, those concerned with human rights abroad all want the national government to spend time and money to champion their preferred foreign policies. Other domestic constituencies may have no interest, pecuniary or otherwise, in international affairs, and would prefer that the national government spend all its efforts on purely local concerns. The conflict, then, may not be so much between domestic and international goals as it is among domestic groups that place different values on the importance of foreign and domestic initiatives.

Either way, policymakers cannot do everything that they, and all their constituents, would like all of the time. They need to choose among a range of options that involve trade-offs on many dimensions; the international-domestic dimension is crucial to foreign policy. This much is true for all countries, at all times. However, the characteristics of the trade-off—the degree to which foreign initiatives require domestic sacrifice or vice versa—vary widely among countries, and over time.

Two determinants of the constraints on policymakers appear crucial: a country's international capabilities, and its national goals. A country with little ability to affect the rest of the world is strongly constrained by it; a country that can fundamentally alter global conditions is far less constrained. At the same time, policymakers whose people are supremely hostile to involvement in global affairs are limited in what they can do internationally, while those who represent constituents with strong overseas interests may be compelled to play a global role.

In this context, what can be said about the prospects for American foreign policy in today's world? It seems to me—and to an extent this simply involves a reworking of the factors Paarlberg has raised—that there have been major changes in both of the determinants mentioned above, America's international capacity and the domestic support for its global role.

Changed International Capabilities

The more influence a country has over international conditions, the less constrained it is by these conditions. The capacity of very large countries to impose, so to speak, domestic conditions on the rest of the world is easily understood in some realms. The notion of an optimal tariff, for example, depends on the ability of the country imposing it to affect the world price of the good in question. Similarly, large countries may be able to affect global macroeconomic conditions, so that they can "export inflation" or unilaterally raise international interest rates.

As the United States had come to account for a smaller share of world economic activity—whether measured in terms of output, trade, or investment—American conditions have come to exercise less unilateral effect on international conditions. This has necessarily tightened the constraints on American foreign policy: the less domestic conditions can be inflicted on the rest of the world, the likelier it is that domestic circumstances will be forced to conform to global trends.

The United States is facing constraints more similar to those of relatively smaller countries. Most countries are "price-takers" in the world economy; for an extraordinary thirty years after World War II, the United States was something of a "price-maker" in many policy arenas. Now, although the United States remains the single largest actor in the world economy, it is less able to affect the global economy single handedly.

This makes it ever more important that U.S. government policy focus on preparing American society for the international challenges it faces. The costs of American inability to compete in world markets, low levels of American investment, a weak economic infrastructure, and other features of the U.S. economy, are much higher today than they might have been in an earlier era. Resolving these problems is that much more pressing.

Changed National Conditions

While the United States has become less influential on global conditions, the American economy has become substantially more integrated with that of the rest of the world. This is true of most nations and motivates our focus on the problems of "deep integration."

For the United States, contemporary international economic integration represents a dramatic change from prior relative insularity. Although international trade and investment have always been important for some Americans, since the Civil War they have typically represented small shares of total American economic activity. Today the shares are large by American standards, and they have been expanding continually.

The result of this growing American economic integration has been to swell the ranks of those in the United States interested in safeguarding global conditions important to them. The balance of domestic political forces has been shifting, albeit in gradual and halting ways, in favor of those willing to have the United States undertake potentially costly measures at the domestic and international level in order to help preserve global trade and payments. Of course, greater economic openness has also given rise to opposition to openness—witness the NAFTA and GATT debates. However, I believe underlying socioeconomic conditions have significantly altered the political environment to increase the probability that the U.S. government can impose domestic sacrifice on some in the interests of access to and success in the international economy for others.

On both these dimensions, my conclusions parallel those of Paarlberg, especially his insistence on the need to bring American conditions into conformity with global circumstances before attempting bold new international initiatives. However, I believe that the analytical perspective I have suggested is more illuminating than the simple focus on inward and outward priority. It allows us to examine the trend in America's international position and draw conclusions about the constraints on policy—the greater the ability of the United States to affect world conditions, the looser the constraints. It also allows us to investigate the socioeconomic and political balance and its implications for American foreign policy— the stronger the net domestic support for "internationalist" policies, the easier it will be for the U.S. government to undertake them.

Although the difference may seem trivial, I think it does highlight several important features of American foreign policy. The impact of the changed international position of the United States is related to, but not the same as, the impact of changing domestic conditions. The two may indeed interact, but it can be useful to separate them analytically.

For example, in the early postwar period, the United States had extraordinary international capabilities in most realms, but little domestic interest in them. Though a few Americans cared deeply about international conditions, most were less concerned. The country pursued global initiatives only so long as they imposed few costs on the mass of Americans. In comparing the postwar period to the 1990s, it is important to separate out the two sets of changes: the United States is less unilaterally influential than earlier, but there are more domestic interests directly concerned about foreign affairs. Today, although "internationalist" policies have more domestic impact, they also generate more domestic support. These may cut in very different directions, and how they play out depends on the specifics of the policy.

This sort of perspective may lead to different conclusions in different issue areas, regions, and time periods. The United States probably has more unilateral impact on global currency markets than on international banking; more in the Western Hemisphere than in South Asia. And there is probably more domestic support within the United States for trade liberalization than for the harmonization of standards, more for financial integration than for macroeconomic policy coordination.

To put the matter differently, I do not see the choices available to American policymakers as Paarlberg does, as a trade-off between inward-first and outward-first policies. I *do* think that there are other crucial choices to be made, especially about bearing domestic costs for international purposes and vice versa. These choices are always present for all countries, but the relative costs and benefits change across countries and over time. They have changed substantially for the United States in the past thirty years. The example of American monetary policy is illustrative.

In the late 1960s and early 1970s, American macroeconomic policies were at odds with those of its major trading partners. The overwhelming size of the U.S. economy and the central role of the U.S. dollar meant that the United States had the capacity to force the rest of the world to adjust to its concerns. The relative unimportance of American international trade and investment to the domestic economy in the early 1970s, at the same time, meant that there was little domestic support for undertaking domestic adjustment for international reasons. The result was that the United States was able and willing to force its allies to accept a unilateral initiative to effectively break up the monetary order that had reigned until 1971.

Since then, both American capabilities and American domestic politics have changed. The attempts of the late 1970s to stimulate the domestic economy regardless of the international consequences ran into the greater influence of Europe and Japan and the growing concern of American economic agents about the implications of the dollar losing international credibility. The attempts of the early and middle 1980s to pursue monetary and fiscal policies at odds with the rest of the world gave rise to significant domestic costs as the dollar appreciation subjected American producers to competitive pressure and raised the specter of protectionism. At the same time, America's monetary-fiscal mix led to complaints by European and Japanese leaders that were much more difficult to ignore than those that preceded the 1971 Nixon shock.

The diminished ability of the United States to carry out international initiatives unilaterally and the growing international economic integration of the United States create strong incentives for policymakers to bring American conditions into line with the country's international economic position. Certainly countervailing pressures, to shunt costly adjustments overseas and to shelter domestic producers from foreign competition, remain powerful. But the prospects for continued American international engagement, and leadership, depend upon the ways in which policymakers respond to changed and changing international and domestic constraints.

The Way Forward

I conclude in strong agreement with Robert Paarlberg on his fundamental point. America's international position depends first and foremost on decisions made at the domestic level, about domestic conditions. No country's leadership can long engage its people in foreign endeavors they believe to be unjustifiable. No country can enter into fruitful relations with other countries when it is unable to carry out the terms of its commitments.

Paarlberg and I may have different perspectives on how to think about the determinants of these decisions and about the impact of global and local trends on them. Here I would ask for more clarity in his definition of terms, a rethinking of some of his categories, and a more explicit presentation of the logic and evidence underlying his policy recommendations.

However, these differences should not obscure the fact that in its central point and recommendation Robert Paarlberg's essay is persuasive. Paarlberg is certainly right that whatever leadership the United States will exercise in world affairs will have to begin at home.

References

Anderson, Kym, and Yujiro Hayami. 1986. *The Political Economy of Agricultural Protection.* London: Allen and Unwin.

Auletta, Ken. 1993. "Raiding the Global Village." *New Yorker,* August 2:25–30.

Benedick, Richard Elliot. 1991. *Ozone Diplomacy: New Directions in Safeguarding the Planet.* Harvard University Press.

Bergsten, C. Fred. 1992. "The Primacy of Economics." *Foreign Policy* 87(Summer):3–24.

Bergsten, C. Fred, and Henry R. Nau. 1985. "The State of the Debate: Reaganomics." *Foreign Policy* 59 (Summer): 132–53.

Bergsten, C. Fred, and Marcus Noland. 1993. *Reconcilable Differences? United States-Japan Economic Conflict.* Washington: Institute for International Economics.

Brown, Seyom. 1988. *New Forces, Old Forces, and the Future of World Politics.* Glenview, Ill.: Scott, Foresman.

Bryant, Ralph C. Forthcoming. *International Coordination of National Stabilization Policies.* Brookings.

Califano, Joseph A., Jr. 1994. "Imperial Congress." *New York Times Magazine,* January 23:40–41.

Clinton, Gov. Bill, and Sen. Al Gore. 1992. *Putting People First.* Times Books.

Clinton, President William J., and Vice President Albert Gore, Jr. 1993. "The Climate Change Action Plan." (October). Executive Office of the President.

Clough, Michael. 1994. "Grass-Roots Policymaking: Say Good-Bye to the 'Wise Men.'" *Foreign Affairs* 73 (January-February):2–7.

Cohen, Stephen D. 1982. "Approaches to the International Economic Policy-Making Process." In *America in a Changing World Political Economy,* edited by William P. Avery and David P. Rapkin, 147–74. Longman.

Cooper, Richard N. 1972–73. "Trade Policy Is Foreign Policy." *Foreign Policy* 9 (Winter):18–36.

Cowhey, Peter F. 1993. "Domestic Institutions and the Credibility of International Commitments: Japan and the United States." *International Organization* 47(2):299–326.

Dertouzos, Michael L., and others. 1989. *Made in America: Regaining the Productive Edge.* MIT Press.

Destler, I. M. *American Trade Politics,* 2d ed. 1992. Washington: Institute for International Economics.

Destler, I. M., and C. Randall Henning. 1989. *Dollar Politics: Exchange Rate Policymaking in the United States.* Washington: Institute for International Economics.

Dobson, Wendy. 1991. *Economic Policy Coordination: Requiem or Prologue?* Washington: Institute for International Economics.

Ek, Carl W., and Charles E. Hanrahan. 1991. "Agricultural Commodity and Trade Policy: The Farm Bill, the Budget, and the GATT." CRS Report for Congress 91–200 RCO. Washington: Congressional Research Service.

Epstein, Susan B., and Carl W. Ek. 1992. "Agricultural GATT Triggers." CRS Report for Congress 92–343 ENR. (April 7). Washington: Congressional Research Service.

Feldstein, Martin. 1988. "Distinguished Lecture on Economics in Government: Thinking about International Economic Coordination." *Journal of Economic Perspectives* 2 (Spring): 3–13.

———ed. 1988. *International Economic Coordination.* University of Chicago Press.

Frankel, Jeffrey A. 1988. *Obstacles to International Macroeconomic Policy Coordination.* Princeton Studies in International Finance, No. 64. Princeton University, International Finance Section.

Frankel, Jeffrey A., and Katherine E. Rockett. 1988. "International Macroeconomic Policy Coordination When Policymakers Do Not Agree on the True Model." *American Economic Review* 78(June):318–40.

Friedman, Benjamin M. 1989. *Day of Reckoning: The Consequences of American Economic Policy.* Vintage.

Garten, Jeffrey E. 1992. *A Cold Peace: America, Japan, Germany, and the Struggle for Supremacy.* Random House.

Gilpin, Robert. 1977. "Economic Interdependence and National Security in Historical Perspective." In *Economic Issues and National Security,* edited by Klaus Knorr and Frank N. Trager, 19–66. Lawrence, Kans.: Regents Press of Kansas.

Gore, Vice President Al. 1993. *Earth in the Balance: Ecology and the Human Spirit.* New York: Plume.

Hastedt, Glenn P., and Anthony J. Eksterowicz. 1993. "Presidential Leadership in the Post–Cold War Era." *Presidential Studies Quarterly* 23(3):445–58.

Heclo, Hugh. 1977. *A Government of Strangers: Executive Politics in Washington.* Brookings.

Henning, C. Randall. 1994. *Currencies and Politics in the United States, Germany, and Japan.* Washington: Institute for International Economics.

Hoffmann, Stanley. 1968. *Gulliver's Troubles, Or the Setting of American Foreign Policy.* McGraw-Hill.

———. 1993. "French Dilemmas and Strategies in the New Europe," In *After the Cold War: International Institutions and State Strategies in Europe, 1989–91,* edited by Robert O. Keohane, Joseph S. Nye, and Stanley Hoffmann, 127–147. Harvard University Press.

Huntington, Samuel P. 1981. *American Politics: The Promise of Disharmony.* Harvard University Press.

Ikenberry, G. John. 1988. "Conclusion: An Institutional Approach to American Foreign Economic Policy." *International Organization* 42(1):219–243.

———. 1993. "Salvaging the G-7." *Foreign Affairs* 72 (Spring):132–139.

James, Scott C., and David A. Lake. 1989. "The Second Face of Hegemony: Britain's Repeal of the Corn Laws and the American Walker Tariff of 1846." *International Organization* 43(1):1–29.

Katzenstein, Peter J. 1985. *Small States in World Markets: Industrial Policy in Europe.* Cornell University Press.

Kaufman, Burton Ira, ed. 1969. *Washington's Farewell Address: The View from the 20th Century.* Chicago: Quadrangle Books.

Keohane, Robert O. 1984. *After Hegemony: Cooperation and Discord in the World Political Economy.* Princeton University Press.

Kissinger, Henry A. 1965. *The Troubled Partnership: A Re-appraisal of the Atlantic Alliance.* McGraw-Hill.

Krasner, Stephen D. 1982. "American Policy and Global Economic Stability." In *America in a Changing World Political Economy,* edited by William P. Avery and David P. Rapkin, 29–48. Longman.

Lanier, Robin. 1993. "Tariff Cuts and the Budget Deal." *Journal of Commerce,* July 16:6A.

Lawrence, Richard. 1993. "Nafta Talks to Continue until Agreement Reached." *Journal of Commerce,* August 4:2A.

Lowi, Theodore J. 1979. *The End of Liberalism: The Second Republic of the United States.* 2d ed. W. W. Norton & Company.

Malabre, Alfred L., Jr. 1987. *Beyond Our Means: How Reckless Borrowing Now Threatens to Overwhelm Us.* Random House.

Manning, Bayliss. 1977. "The Congress, the Executive, and Intermestic Affairs: Three Proposals." *Foreign Affairs* 55(2):306–324.

Martin, Pierre. 1993. "Redefining Fair Trade: Issue Coalitions and the Politics of U.S. Trade Unilateralism, 1981–88." Paper prepared for the annual meeting of the International Studies Association, Acapulco, Mexico, March 23–27.

Milner, Helen. 1993. "Maintaining International Commitments in Trade Policy," In *Do Institutions Matter? Government Capabilities in the United States and Abroad,* edited by R. Kent Weaver and Bert A. Rockman, 345–369. Brookings.

Moran, Theodore H. 1993. "An Economics Agenda for Neorealists." *International Security* 18(Fall):211–215.

Murphy, Craig N. 1994. *International Organization and Industrial Change: Global Governance Since 1850.* Cambridge: Polity Press.

Nau, Henry R. 1985. "Where Reaganomics Works." *Foreign Policy* 57 (Winter 1984–85):14–37.

———. 1990. *The Myth of America's Decline: Leading the World Economy into the 1990s.* Oxford University Press.

Nelson, Mark M., Peter S. Rashish. 1993. "Europe: Clinton's Missing Link." *Journal of Commerce,* March 26:8A.

Nivola, Pietro S. 1993. *Regulating Unfair Trade.* Brookings.

Nye, Joseph S., Jr. 1990. *Bound to Lead: The Changing Nature of American Power.* Basic Books.

O'Connor, Karen, and Larry J. Sabato. 1994. *American Government: Roots and Reform.* Macmillan.

Organization for Economic Cooperation and Development (OECD). 1992. *OECD Economic Surveys: Japan 1991/92.* Paris.

———. 1993. *Main Economic Indicators, May 1993.* Statistics Directorate. Paris.

Owen, Henry. 1994. "Targeting the Middle Class: That's Where the Money Is." *Foreign Affairs* 73 (January-February):168–72.

Paarlberg, Robert L. 1988. *Fixing Farm Trade: Policy Options for the United States.* Cambridge: Ballinger.

———. 1990. "The Mysterious Popularity of EEP." *Choices* 5 (Second Quarter):14–17.

———. 1992a. "How Agriculture Blocked the Uruguay Round." *SAIS Review* 12(1):27–42.

———. 1992b. "Ecodiplomacy: U.S. Environmental Policy Goes Abroad." In *Eagle in a New World: American Grand Strategy in the Post-Cold War Era*, edited by Kenneth A. Oye, Robert J. Lieber, and Donald Rothchild, 207–231. HarperCollins.

Parson, Edward A. 1993. "Protecting the Ozone Layer." In *Institutions for the Earth: Sources of Effective International Environmental Protection*, edited by Peter M. Haas, Robert O. Keohane, and Marc A. Levy, 27–73. MIT Press.

Pastor, Robert A. 1980. *Congress and the Politics of U.S. Foreign Economic Policy, 1929–76.* University of California Press.

Peterson, Peter G. 1993. "Facing Up." *Atlantic Monthly* 272(4):77–90.

Pharr, Susan J., and Joseph L. Badaracco, Jr. 1986. "Coping with Crisis: Environmental Regulation," In *America Versus Japan*, edited by Thomas K. McCraw, 229–59. Boston: Harvard Business School Press.

Porter, Roger B. 1982. "Organizing International Economic Policy Making." In *America in a Changing World Political Economy*, edited by William P. Avery and David P. Rapkin, 175–190. Longman.

Porter, Roger B., and Raymond Vernon. 1989. *Foreign Economic Policymaking in the United States: An Approach for the 1990s.* Harvard University, John F. Kennedy School of Government.

Prestowitz, Clyde V., Jr. 1989. *Trading Places: How We Are Giving Our Future to Japan and How to Reclaim It.* Basic Books.

Putnam, Robert D. 1988. "Diplomacy and Domestic Politics: The Logic of Two-Level Games." *International Organization* 42(3):427–60.

Rapp, David. 1988. *How the U.S. Got Into Agriculture and Why It Can't Get Out.* Washington: Congressional Quarterly.

Reich, Robert B. 1992. *The Work of Nations: Preparing Ourselves for 21st Century Capitalism.* Vintage Books.

Rivlin, Alice M. 1992. *Reviving the American Dream: The Economy, the States, and the Federal Government.* Brookings.

Rogowski, Ronald. 1989. *Commerce and Coalitions: How Trade Affects Domestic Political Alignments.* Princeton University Press.

Roningen, Vernon O., and Praveen M. Dixit. 1989. "Economic Implications of Agricultural Policy Reforms in Industrial Market Economies." AGES 89-36.

U.S. Department of Agriculture, Economic Research Service, Agriculture and Trade Analysis Division.

Rostow, W. W. 1960. *The Stages of Economic Growth: A Non-Communist Manifesto.* London: Cambridge University Press.

Ruggie, John G. 1982. "International Regimes, Transactions, and Change: Embedded Liberalism in the Postwar Economic Order." *International Organization* 36(Spring):379–415.

Sand, Peter H. 1990. *Lessons Learned in Global Environmental Governance.* Washington: World Resources Institute.

Sanderson, Fred H. 1994. "The GATT Agreement on Agriculture." Discussion Paper Series, January 1994. Washington: National Center for Food and Agricultural Policy.

Schattschneider, E. E. 1935. *Politics, Pressures and the Tariff: A Study of Private Enterprise in Pressure Politics, as Shown in the 1929–1930 Revision of the Tariff.* Prentice-Hall.

Schick, Allen. 1993. "Government versus Budget Deficits." In *Do Institutions Matter? Government Capabilities in the United States and Abroad,* edited by R. Kent Weaver and Bert A. Rockman, 187–236. Brookings.

Shuman, Michael H. 1992. "Dateline Main Street: Courts v. Local Foreign Policies." *Foreign Policy* 86 (Spring):158–77.

Simon, Paul. 1980. *The Tongue-Tied American: Confronting the Foreign Language Crisis.* New York: Continuum.

Spiro, David E. 1993. "Capital and Debt Policy." In *U.S. Foreign Policy: The Search for a New Role,* edited by Robert J. Art and Seyom Brown, 166–91. Macmillan.

Tanzi, Vito. 1989. "International Coordination of Fiscal Policies: Current and Future Issues." In *Fiscal Policy, Economic Adjustment, and Financial Markets,* edited by Mario Monti, 7–37. International Monetary Fund.

Thurow, Lester. 1992. *Head to Head: The Coming Economic Battle among Japan, Europe, and America.* Morrow.

de Tocqueville, Alexis. 1945. *Democracy in America.* Volume I. Vintage Books.

United Nations Development Programme (UNDP). 1993. *Human Development Report 1993.* Oxford University Press.

U.S. Department of Agriculture (USDA). Economic Research Service. 1989. *Western Europe Agriculture and Trade Report.* Report RS-89-2 (July).

———. 1993. *Europe: Situation and Outlook.* Report RS-93-5 (September).

U.S. Department of Agriculture (USDA). Office of Economics. 1992. "Preliminary Analysis of the Economic Implications of the Dunkel Text for American Agriculture." (March).

Vernon, Raymond, Debora L. Spar, and Glenn Tobin. 1991. *Iron Triangles and Revolving Doors: Cases in U.S. Foreign Economic Policymaking.* Praeger.

Vernon, Raymond. 1993. "Behind the Scenes: How Policymaking in the European Community, Japan, and the United States Affects Global Negotiations." *Environment* 35(5):13–20, 35–43.

Woodward, Bob. 1994. *The Agenda.* Simon & Schuster.

Index

Andrew Carnegie Library
Livingstone College
701 W. Monroe St.
Salisbury, NC 28144

126540